D0206257

Boys among Men

Boys among Men
Trying and Sentencing Juveniles as Adults

David L. Myers

Criminal Justice, Delinquency, and Corrections
Marilyn D. McShane and Frank Williams, Series Editors

Westport, Connecticut
London

Library of Congress Cataloging-in-Publication Data

Myers, David L., 1968–
    Boys among men : trying and sentencing juveniles as adults / David L. Myers.
        p. cm. — (Criminal justice, delinquency, and corrections, ISSN 1535–0371)
    Includes bibliographical references and index.
    ISBN 0–275–98254–8 (alk. paper)
    1. Juvenile delinquency—United States. 2. Juvenile delinquents—Legal
status, laws, etc.—United States. 3. Juvenile justice, Administration of—United
States. 4. Criminal justice, Administration of—United States. 5. Criminal
courts—United States. I. Title. II. Series.
HV9104.M94 2005
345.73'05—dc22   2004028153

British Library Cataloguing in Publication Data is available.

Library of Congress Catalog Card Number: 2004028153
ISBN: 0–275–98254–8
ISSN: 1535–0371

First published in 2005

Praeger Publishers, 88 Post Road West, Westport, CT 06881
An imprint of Greenwood Publishing Group, Inc.
www.praeger.com

Printed in the United States of America

The paper used in this book complies with the
Permanent Paper Standard issued by the National
Information Standards Organization (Z39.48–1984).

10 9 8 7 6 5 4 3 2 1

To Bryce, Abby, and Nicole—
You keep me going.

Contents

Series Foreword

Cases like this seem to appear frequently in the news. A 10-year-old faces murder charges in the shooting of his father in Harris County, Texas. The maximum 40-year term he faces is just another challenge in his already difficult life. The boy struggled through his parents' angry marriage, their long and bitter divorce complete with charges of sexual abuse, split custody and stepfamilies. He was on Prozac and being shuttled from one parent to the other when he pulled his mother's handgun from his backpack and shot his father, a prominent physician, in the back. In Texas, 10 is the earliest age at which a child can be officially charged with a crime.

The prosecution of children as adults is a controversial and emotionally laden practice born, many suspect, of get-tough justice and legislative responses to sensationalized media coverage of crimes. What is often overlooked is the much less dramatic accumulation of scientific evidence and data that chronicles exactly how this trend is playing out and what the unintended consequences have been.

This book is a classic example of reality not living up to expectations. It is a careful analysis of each aspect of the policy and its application. This study directs the reader away from the rhetoric and into the daily workings of the transfer decision. This is not only the most comprehensive and up-to-date look at the outcome of transferring juveniles to adult court and subjecting them to adult sentences, it is a perfect case study of how even a well-intentioned goal can be corrupted.

A copy of this work should be laid on the desk of every legislator and policymaker. They should be challenged to address the findings, and even more so, they should be held accountable should they fail to do so. In an era when it is obvious that we have "left many children behind," we should be much more concerned about where we have left them and the damage that has been done by leaving them where we did.

Marilyn D. McShane
Frank P. Williams
Series Editors

Acknowledgments

There are several people I would like to thank for helping me complete this book. First, my editors, Marilyn McShane and Suzanne Staszak-Silva—your patience and guidance are deeply appreciated. Next, my graduate assistant, Rebecca Boyd, and my secretary, Debbie Mock— your proofreading and suggestions improved the quality of my work. Third, to my family, friends, and students, thanks for putting up with me.

Finally, I would like to thank Leo Balk of LFB Scholarly Publishing for permission to use some of my work previously published in *Excluding Violent Youths from Juvenile Court: The Effectiveness of Legislative Waiver* (2001). Specifically, some information contained in Chapters 3, 5, and 7 appeared in this prior work; the current chapters contain updated and expanded information and discussion.

CHAPTER 1

"Adult Crime, Adult Time"

On October 29, 1997, Nathaniel Abraham shot and killed 18-year-old Ronnie Green outside a convenience store in Pontiac, Michigan.[1] Abraham apparently did not know Green, who was shot from about 300 feet away with a stolen .22-caliber rifle. The assailant was arrested two days later, was subsequently tried on murder charges, and was convicted. He then received a lengthy sentence of incarceration in a correctional facility. Aside from defense claims that the shooting was accidental, the facts of the case essentially were indisputable, and this type of murder often would not generate anything more than local interest. The convicted killer, however, was less than 5 feet tall, weighed about 65 pounds, and was 11 years old when the shooting occurred. Despite these characteristics, he was prosecuted as an adult criminal defendant.

The case of Nathaniel Abraham, which drew both national and international attention, came at a time when youth violence had become a top nationwide concern. Throughout much of the 1990s, both during and after years of rising juvenile violent crime arrest rates, news stories routinely portrayed seemingly senseless acts of violence committed by young people.[2] These accounts often involved guns, drugs, gangs, or all three, and viewers and readers generally were left with the impression that children and adolescents were out of control, the juvenile justice system was incapable of handling the situation, and therefore something should be done to deal with these dangerous youths.

In response to this state of affairs, nearly all states had moved to strengthen the procedures and sanctions available for handling serious and violent juvenile offenders by the time of Nathaniel Abraham's arrest. The most popular approach was to pass laws that eased the process of transferring (also known as waiving, certifying, or remanding)[3] adolescents to adult criminal court.[4] This transfer movement appeared to be fueled by strong public support; in general, many citizens seemed to believe that youthful offenders were "getting off easy" in juvenile court and that this lenient treatment was contributing greatly to high levels of juvenile crime.[5] In the adult system, it was thought, serious and violent youths would be held more accountable and would receive harsher punishment. This, in turn, would have a beneficial impact on juvenile crime by providing stronger retribution, greater deterrence, and longer incapacitation.

Unfortunately, changes in juvenile waiver policies, whereby juvenile offenders are waived, or transferred, to adult courts, were not guided by systematic research and careful planning. In the mid-1980s, prior to the surge in youth violence, internationally known criminologist David Farrington and colleagues discussed what was known at that time about the effectiveness of treating juvenile offenders as adults:

> It is not at all certain that we gain increased deterrence, retribution, or incapacitation in this way. Youth committed by the adult court to adult prisons might become hardened and more, rather than less, likely to offend again upon release. What is needed is much more careful research following comparable samples of offenders through these different experiences to provide a better understanding and confident policies about the division of jurisdiction between the two courts, the relative effectiveness of the dispositional options they provide, and the efficacy of the criteria used to select offenders for differential processing and disposition.[6]

About 10 years later, near the peak of the youth violence epidemic and resultant waiver movement, well-known juvenile justice and delinquency prevention expert James Howell asserted that "it is surprising how little information is available on criminal justice system handling of juvenile offenders.... Transfer is a socio-legal policy based on very little information."[7] His review of the literature found the relevant research to be generally of uneven quality, with few studies available that actually conducted a meaningful comparison of the effectiveness of juvenile and adult court processing. The research that did exist did not overall support certification to adult court as meeting its overall goals. However, this lack of empirical evidence and scientific support did not prevent states from rapidly adopting transfer laws that sought to place greater numbers of juvenile offenders into the adult criminal justice system.

As this book is being written, modern waiver laws and policies are still in place and much more is known about their effectiveness (and ineffectiveness) in dealing with youthful offenders. The topic of juvenile transfer in the United States has produced much debate and, in recent times, many questions about its efficacy. By assessing the information and evidence that is available, an attempt will be made to bring understanding to this controversial practice that continues to be important in the operation of both the juvenile and adult justice systems. First, we will consider how and why waiving juveniles to adult court came to be such a popular strategy and then examine a framework for considering the variety of issues associated with its use.

CONTEMPORARY CONCERNS ABOUT YOUTH VIOLENCE

During the past several decades, juveniles younger than age 18 have accounted for roughly one third of all serious property crime arrests and less than one fifth of all serious violent crime arrests in America.[8] More than two thirds of all juvenile arrests are for nonindex crimes (that is, offenses other than murder, rape, robbery, aggravated assault, burglary, larceny, motor vehicle theft, and arson). Furthermore, of the total population of juveniles in America, only about 6% are arrested each year and less than 1% of this population are arrested for a violent offense. Despite these aggregate statistics, from the mid-1980s to the mid-1990s a disturbing trend in juvenile offending emerged that heightened public fears and greatly contributed to a variety of changes in juvenile justice.

Prior to the mid-1980s, official juvenile violent crime arrest rates were relatively stable for roughly a 15-year period.[9] By the late 1980s and early 1990s, however, youth violence had emerged as a major public and political issue. Concerns were raised based on both the rising level and lethality of violent acts committed by and against young people. Between

1985 and 1994, the juvenile violent crime arrest rate increased by about 75%.[10] While juvenile arrest rates for robbery and aggravated assault surged dramatically, the murder arrest rate of juveniles more than doubled. Moreover, these increases in offending corresponded with a similar upswing in violent crime victimization among youths, and firearm use appeared to be a key aspect of these trends.[11] Interestingly, in contrast to rising juvenile violent crime, the arrest rate for juvenile property crimes did not increase substantially during the same time period. Although a modest increase occurred from 1989 to 1991, by 1993 the rate was at nearly the same level as it was from 1985 to 1989.[12]

Juvenile Population Changes

By the mid-1990s, it was clear that the United States was experiencing an epidemic of youth violence. As summarized by Mark Moore and Michael Tonry in a comprehensive review of American youth violence, many commentators and researchers offered a variety of explanations for why this epidemic occurred.[13] To begin, crime rates are age-sensitive. It is well established that involvement in most types of crime peaks during adolescence and young adulthood and steadily declines thereafter.[14] This fact has been used to explain at least partially the dramatic increases in official crime that occurred from the mid-1960s to the mid-1970s, when post-World War II "baby boomers" reached their crime-prone years. Similar to this previous time period, the size and share of the U.S. population that was youthful grew between 1985 and 1995 as "echo boom" children started to reach adolescence. This increase in the juvenile population no doubt played a role in rising levels of youth violence and in youth violence becoming a larger share of overall violence.

It was not just that the size of the juvenile population increased, however; violent offending and victimization rates within this group rose to historically unprecedented levels. It is possible that a larger juvenile population is harder to supervise, manage, and train or that increased numbers of adolescents and young adults can influence and shape the larger American culture, which seems to have occurred in the mid-to-late 1960s. In any event, an explanation of rising youth violence rates based on the age distribution of the population requires a consideration of both the size of the juvenile population and the effects that a larger group of young people can have on society.

Risk and Protective Factors

A second explanation for the youth violence epidemic focuses on the circumstances under which contemporary youths have been raised. During the past 20 years, a great deal of research has been conducted on "risk factors" and "protective factors" that predict juvenile delinquency and violent offending.[15] In general, risk factors are negative characteristics that can exist at the individual, family, school, and community levels, and they are associated with higher amounts of adolescent problem behaviors. Protective factors, on the other hand, are positive life circumstances operating at the same four levels and are associated with lower amounts of adolescent behavioral problems.

The extent to which youths were experiencing greater risk (for example, poverty, poor family cohesion, or availability of drugs and alcohol) and lesser protection (for example, weak bonds with parents, lack of social skills, or unclear standards for behavior) during the 1980s and early 1990s may help explain the corresponding rise in violent youthful offending and victimization. This reasoning seems applicable particularly for poor, inner-city, minority youths who were (and still are) highly over-represented in violent crime arrest statistics and in experiencing more risk factors and fewer protective factors.[16] Recent research on the effectiveness of prevention and intervention programs that seek to decrease risk factors and enhance protective factors provides further support for this notion.[17] The growing use of these programs in the past decade also might help explain overall declines in youth violence since the mid-1990s.

Culture of Violence

A third explanation discussed by Moore and Tonry emphasizes the emergence of a new culture of violence in America.[18] Many have suggested that violence in modern television shows, movies, video games, and sports is to blame for a variety of juvenile acts ranging from random assaults in public places to planned shootings in schools. This view holds that youths have been socialized into violence from an early age, which subsequently impacts on their adolescent behavior. This broad cultural explanation might help account for the onset and continuation of the mid-1980s to mid-1990s youth violence epidemic but not the declines in violent juvenile arrest rates that have occurred since the mid-1990s (as media violence appears to be more pervasive now than it was 10 years ago). From a cultural perspective, more local and quickly changing cultural influences, such as gangs, drug markets, and schools, might provide better explanations for the rising and falling levels of youth violence.[19]

Drugs and Guns

Two additional, intertwined explanations for the surge in youth violence also merit attention. These focus on the corresponding crack cocaine epidemic and the rising prevalence and use of firearms among young people. It is noteworthy that "the crack cocaine epidemic occurred at times and places where the epidemic of youth violence occurred."[20] These two occurrences can be linked based on the idea that a capacity for violence is an important asset for those involved in illegal drug markets and that youths using cocaine might be more violent either because of the intoxication or because violence is needed to obtain money to buy the drug. However, the crack cocaine explanation alone is limited, as violence committed by youths actually is not that strongly connected to either cocaine dealing or cocaine use.[21] There is stronger evidence that guns and gangs play a large role in the relationship that exists between violence and drugs.[22]

The youth violence epidemic was marked by large increases in gun homicides and in weapons law violations.[23] While the supply or flow of weapons to youths may have generally increased, it seems more likely that the demand for guns among young people rose who were recruited into drug markets and gangs and experienced a more violent culture overall.[24] The increasing supply and demand for guns among adolescents no doubt contributed to the frequency and seriousness of violent acts by youthful offenders and against similarly aged victims. Furthermore, violent acts, particularly gun homicides, by young people often are committed against strangers as well as acquaintances and family members, which is instrumental in generating public fear and feelings of vulnerability.

Predictions, Panic, and Policy Changes

Of course, no single explanation for the increase in youth violence appears sufficient; it is likely that all of these factors contributed in some way, both alone and in conjunction with one another. Moreover, in addition to rising juvenile violent crime arrest rates and increasing public concern, in the mid-1990s one other factor greatly added to a perceived need to "do something" about youth violence—the sheer number of young people. Not only had the population of juveniles been growing but this group was expected to continue to expand for at least the next 15 years. When combined with high levels of violent offending, the enlarging juvenile population played a role in numerous dire predictions. In 1994, for example, the National Council on Crime and Delinquency suggested that if juvenile violent crime rates continued to increase as they had from the mid-1980s to that point, by the year 2002 total juvenile arrests could rise by more than 100%.[25] These predictions further incited already heightened fears about youth violence. Alarmed politicians and even criminologists warned that we needed to "get ready."[26] Authors such as Bennett, DiIulio, and Walters placed the blame for increased juvenile violence on the youths themselves, painting a grim and powerful picture:

> Based on all that we have witnessed, researched, and heard from people who are close to the action, here is what we believe: America is now home to thickening ranks of juvenile "super-predators"—radically impulsive, brutally remorseless youngsters, including ever more preteen age boys, who murder, assault, rape, rob, burglarize, deal deadly drugs, join gun-toting gangs, and create serious communal disorders. They do not fear the stigma of arrest, the pains of imprisonment, or the pangs of conscience. They perceive hardly any relationship between doing right (or wrong) now and being rewarded (punished) for it later. To these mean-street youngsters, the words "right" and "wrong" have no fixed moral meaning.[27]

Descriptions of current and future juvenile superpredators[28] flooding the nation's streets were very influential on public policy. From 1992 to 1995, 47 states and the District of Columbia passed laws that sought to address the youth violence problem, and the basic theme of these legislative efforts was "getting tough."[29] In general, these juvenile justice reforms most often focused on issues of confidentiality, sentencing, and jurisdiction.

Concerning issues of confidentiality, most states changed the conditions and procedures of juvenile court hearings that had previously distinguished these operations from those in adult criminal court. This typically involved reducing or eliminating the nonpublic nature of juvenile court hearings, making juvenile court records more open and accessible (often to the public and media), and permitting or requiring juvenile courts to notify school districts about youths charged with or convicted of certain offenses. Also, police in many states were granted authorization to fingerprint and photograph specified youthful offenders as well as to report information to statewide repositories. These things were done in an effort to diminish the privacy traditionally provided to juvenile offenders, under the belief that greater confidentiality was a contributing factor in higher rates of youth violence.

Regarding sentencing practices, some state legislatures acted to remove discretion from juvenile court judicial decisions by requiring mandatory minimum periods of confinement for certain serious or violent offenses and offenders. Other common approaches were to raise the maximum age of the juvenile court's continuing jurisdiction over offenders to allow for longer periods of confinement and supervision or to create the opportunity for "blended sentences" that begin in the juvenile system and carry over to adult correctional facilities once legal adulthood is attained. These reforms reflected the desire for more punitive punishments, but they also maintained juvenile court jurisdiction and the status of an offender as a juvenile.

The final and most popular change occurred in the area of jurisdictional authority. From 1992 through 1997, all but six states enacted or expanded provisions to transfer juvenile offenders to adult criminal court.[30] New laws generally sought to remove larger numbers of serious and violent youths from juvenile court and prosecute them in adult court. Again, these reforms were driven by a desire for harsher punishment and fear of what the future might bring, but the key distinction here was the termination of juvenile court jurisdiction and an offender transformation from juvenile delinquent to adult criminal. Through greater retribution, deterrence, and incapacitation, this strategy was expected to reduce youth violence and ease public fears and concern.

THE TRANSFER MOVEMENT AND PUBLIC SUPPORT

Franklin E. Zimring has asserted that the popularity of modern transfer laws rather than other methods of getting tough is based on both their limited financial costs and the symbolic value that juvenile waiver provides for citizens.[31] Concerning costs, expanded transfer provisions may not require large expenditures if waived youths simply are absorbed into existing adult facilities and services, if the actual number of transferred cases turns out to be relatively small, or if prosecutorial charge reduction results in offenders being returned to the juvenile system. In other words, the cost may not be that great because, despite new laws being passed, few changes in day-to-day justice system operations may actually occur.

Perhaps more important than monetary cost is the symbolic value that transfer to adult court provides to the general public. When young people are charged with serious acts of violence, many citizens might experience conflict between the urge to punish criminals and the desire to protect children and youths. This conflict essentially is resolved by declaring the offender to be no longer a juvenile. By legislatively proclaiming that certain youths who are charged with committing particular crimes should be considered adults, policymakers enable the public to focus on accountability and punishment for criminal behavior. Hence, "adult time for adult crime" is an easy battle cry to invoke.

Evidence of Support

By the early to mid-1990s, the American public appeared convinced that certifying serious and violent juvenile offenders as adults was the correct approach to take. A 1993 USA Today/CNN/Gallup poll found that 73% of the adults surveyed favored adult court processing for violent youths.[32] That same year, similar evidence from a 1991 national public opinion survey was reported by Ira M. Schwartz and colleagues.[33] Their findings indicated that most participants believed that juveniles charged with serious property offenses, selling large quantities of illegal drugs, and, in particular, serious violent crimes should be tried in adult criminal court. However, public opinion did not favor giving juveniles the same sentences as adults or placing them in adult correctional facilities. Respondents with children tended to be less punitive toward juvenile offenders than were adults without children, and, somewhat surprisingly, African-American parents were significantly more likely to support punitive juvenile policies than were parents from other racial and ethnic groups.

Subsequent research in both the United States and Canada suggested that public support for the waiver of serious and violent youthful offenders did not subside during the mid-1990s.[34] Again, though, there was little backing for placing adolescents in the same facilities as adults, and a youth's age was found to play an important role, as survey respondents were less likely to desire the transfer of younger juveniles. Furthermore, support for waiving youths was not the result solely of a preference for more punitive punishments; instead, perceptions that other alternatives were ineffective seemed to be an important contributor to public opinion. Still, even during the height of the youth violence epidemic, public opinion research revealed continuing and often high support for juvenile rehabilitation programs and early intervention efforts, with a preference for waiver to adult court generally reserved for older and the most serious and violent offenders.[35]

It is clear that at the same time that states were enacting legislation to facilitate the transfer of juvenile offenders to adult criminal court, citizens generally supported these efforts. It also seems, though, that many modern waiver laws went beyond what the public actually favored. Rather than focusing on older adolescents, many statutes lowered minimum age requirements to include younger teens and even offenders in their pre-teenage years.[36] In addition, similar efforts were made to certify those youth charged with lesser offenses against persons as well as drug, weapons, and property offenses of moderate severity. Finally, many waived offenders face short- or long-term imprisonment in adult correctional facilities as well as lengthy periods of supervision by the criminal justice system while on probation or parole.[37] During this time, the treatment and rehabilitation services they receive often may be of lower quality and effectiveness compared to programs offered by the juvenile system.[38]

WHERE DO WE GO FROM HERE?

There is both good and bad news. Since 1994, juvenile violent crime arrest rates and juvenile rates of arrest for serious property crime have declined steadily.[39] Current juvenile arrest rates for murder, rape, robbery, burglary, and larceny are lower than they were in the mid-1980s, and similar substantial decreases have occurred for aggravated assault, motor vehicle theft, arson, and weapons law violations. By all appearances, the youth violence epidemic ended by the turn of the century, and, in the wake of September 11, 2001, concerns about terrorism and homeland security have taken priority over other social issues.

Waiver laws and policies implemented in the 1990s are still in place, though, and some proponents have given them credit for the recent downturn in serious and violent juvenile offending. As compared to 10 years ago, much more is known, in fact, about the effectiveness of transfer in dealing with young offenders as well as the utility of other prevention and intervention efforts. Considering that the size of the juvenile population in the United States is projected to grow for the next 25 years and that the population of adolescents will soon reach a level similar to that of the mid-1970s,[40] there is good reason for continuing attention to be given to youthful offending and society's response. Moreover, it is quite possible that with funding and other resources directed elsewhere, youth violence will reemerge as a significant social problem, and waiver to adult court again could be viewed as the principal solution.

In this context, an effort will be made in the following chapters to provide greater awareness and knowledge about a practice that continues to have an impact on the operation of both the juvenile and adult justice systems as well as the young offenders contained therein. In seeking to achieve this goal, I will draw on my own research in Pennsylvania during the last six years and the substantial body of literature that has accrued on this topic during the past 30 years. In the end, I will make an argument that transferring juveniles to adult court is a very limited approach to dealing with serious and violent youthful offending and one that should not be fully relied upon by politicians and the general public as a way to prevent and reduce juvenile crime.

In the next two chapters, a history of the evolution of juvenile transfer to adult court will be provided. The notion of distinguishing juvenile delinquents from adult criminals is examined in Chapter 2, along with the development of separate systems of justice for these youths. Chapter 3 considers historical efforts to send certain young offenders to adult court, both prior to and during the previously discussed youth violence epidemic. A case study of transfer practices in Pennsylvania will be presented as an example of what commonly took place at the legislative level in the course of the modern waiver movement.

The case processing of transferred youths is an important contemporary issue to consider. In Chapter 4, the demographic, legal, and social characteristics of certified offenders are inspected, along with the various forms of discretion that are built into transfer proceedings. The case of Nathaniel Abraham will be revisited here to demonstrate both the characteristics of juveniles commonly waived to adult court and the discretionary decision-making that occurs even under recently enacted transfer laws. Chapter 5 then focuses on the stages and results of court processing experienced by waived offenders, particularly in comparison to similar adolescents in juvenile court. We will see that research findings on the case processing outcomes of transferred youths are not always as would be expected by proponents of this approach.

The subsequent two chapters will focus on public protection achieved through juvenile transfer, or whether citizens actually are better protected through expanded waiver laws. Chapter 6 considers the nature and use of punishment and rehabilitation in modern juvenile and criminal justice systems, with an emphasis on the correctional sanctions and services provided to serious and violent youthful offenders. A case study of the State Correctional Institute at Pine Grove, a prison in Pennsylvania designed for violent youths convicted and sentenced by adult courts, will be presented to illustrate recent efforts to address this population of offenders. In Chapter 7, the general and specific deterrent effects of formal punishments are inspected. Further attention is given to the expected deterrent effects of transferring juveniles to adult court. Again, research findings concerning public protection attained through juvenile transfer often are not supportive of this practice.

Finally, the last chapter of the book is devoted to considering several current issues surrounding juvenile transfer and to understanding where this practice might be headed in the future. Recent trends in youth violence, growing knowledge about adolescent development, and the effectiveness of various prevention and intervention efforts will be contemplated along with the issue of imposing capital punishment on juveniles and recent proposals to further reform and even abolish the juvenile court. Chapter 9 concludes with the position that as long as we continue to have separate juvenile and adult justice systems, there will always be a desire and need for transferring some youths to adult court. However, this should be done on a much more limited basis than typically is supported by policymakers and citizens, and greater resources and funding need to be directed at prevention and early intervention strategies that have been shown to be effective in reducing serious and violent juvenile offending.

CHAPTER 2

Separating the Men from the Boys

The term "juvenile delinquency" commonly is used in American society in discussions of why children and youths break the law and what should be done about it. In general, young people are viewed as being distinctly different from adults, including those young children who commit crimes. Although exceptions are made, particularly in cases of serious violent offending, juveniles who break the law are thought to deserve separate consideration than that given to adult criminals. This is such common knowledge that relatively few people would know, in fact, that the concept of delinquency is actually less than 200 years old and that throughout a great deal of American and European history, children were not treated much differently than adults. This is not to suggest that children and youths did not exhibit delinquent behavior until more modern times. There is good evidence that during the Middle Ages and from the 1500s through the 1700s, young people consumed alcohol and drugs, experienced considerable sexual freedoms, carried and used a variety of weapons, and committed various violent acts.[1] It was not until the 1800s, though, that these behaviors became cause for serious concern. Moreover, rather than the deeds of juveniles becoming worse and generating increased alarm, it appears that changes occurred in the way society defined and reacted to these behaviors. This implies that delinquency is a relatively recent social invention and also one that can vary significantly from time to time.

With this information in mind, we will briefly examine the history of childhood, the creation of delinquency, and the development of a separate system of justice for juvenile offenders. Having an understanding of this information is important in examining the topic of juvenile transfer to adult court because this policy essentially transforms delinquent youths into adult criminals to be processed in the criminal (rather than juvenile) justice system. Indeed, an argument could be made that we have somewhat returned to a time when the behavior of children was equated with that of adults and society's response to individual behavior was not that much different based on the individual's age.

THE CONCEPT OF CHILDHOOD

To have a concept of juvenile delinquency, there must first be some agreement that children are different from adults. In America and many other Western nations, for instance, there has been an overall tendency toward an increasing "child-centeredness" in family and social life.[2] Childrearing is viewed as a primary function of the family unit, and children are believed to possess distinctive characteristics and needs that require attention in the execution of proper childrearing practices. Furthermore, this emphasis on the importance of childhood usually is seen as being for the benefit of all society, not just the children themselves. These beliefs are so strong that many people likely would think that they always have been in existence and never will change. A look at history, however, suggests that the notion of childhood is fairly recent in origin and has had an inclination to adjust over time.

Indifference to Children

Historical accounts generally indicate that prior to the year 1400, there was little or no acknowledgment of childhood.[3] This means that although children existed, they were given few special considerations. Infanticide and abandonment frequently were practiced for a variety of reasons (for example, illegitimacy, physical and mental imperfections, too much crying), and boys were valued much more than girls. Those young children who were allowed to live and who needed to be fed and cared for received only cursory acknowledgment from their parents. In fact, children of more affluent parents often were cared for by wet nurses, many of whom accepted too many babies to be able to provide proper nourishment and supervision. Once children were old enough to feed and generally care for themselves, which was no small accomplishment, they were treated as regular people, like everyone else.

There were exceptions to this state of childhood affairs. There is evidence, for example, that in Greece and Rome distinct stages of life were accepted in early civilizations and during medieval times.[4] Furthermore, some bonds of affection between parents and children have existed throughout history, even if they were not that well defined or given great importance. However, as a result of high fertility of mothers combined with high infant mortality (generally caused by disease and poor living conditions), children often were treated with indifference prior to the last several hundred years. Because many or most children would die, strong emotional attachments were risky. Essentially, babies were easily produced, but a child typically had to live a number of years before being viewed as a real person. As Thomas Bernard notes in *The Cycle of Juvenile Justice*:

> This way of "seeing" children was not due to ignorance or evil, but to the terrible conditions under which people lived: most of these children would die and there was nothing you could do. Only when children were 5 or 6 would you begin to assume that they would live, so that you could become attached to them. Before that, it was simply too dangerous.[5]

Signs of Change

Soon after 1400, as living conditions improved and infant mortality began to decline, parents started to recognize and become attached to their children at younger ages. Children even began to be viewed as sources of pleasure and joy. Still, it remained unclear if a particular child would grow into adulthood. Furthermore, no strong attempts were made to shape children's lives for the future, except in the case where a young person was fortunate enough to receive sound apprenticeship training. In addition, communal living and lifestyles were popular; the moral rules of this time allowed many children to be used for adult sexual gratification, and promiscuity at an early age was encouraged.[6] Finally, harsh physical punishments commonly were used in an attempt to control children and secure their obedience. So, although an idea of childhood was emerging, it was much different than the prevalent view of today.

By 1600 (following the Renaissance), there were stronger indicators of change, and the future of children as adults began to be given more attention. Further decreases in the infant mortality rate corresponded in time with growing concerns about the abuse and neglect of children, and reformers who criticized the traditional treatment of children "argued that children required discipline and guidance, not exploitation or indulgence."[7] These views originally were espoused by a relatively small group of moralists and teachers who stressed the importance of formal education and the role of parents in raising their children. These individuals assumed that human nature was fundamentally evil and that by adulthood behavior was too well established to allow for change. However, children could be shaped and molded if proper childrearing techniques were used in a consistent and timely manner.

Children in Colonial America

The emerging notion of childhood became particularly evident in colonial America under the influence of Puritanism.[8] Increasing emphasis was placed on family life and childrearing, and parents were expected to instill a fear of God and respect for authority that would ensure law-abiding behavior and an orderly society. Manuals and books on the topic of proper childrearing were written and circulated, stressing the importance of supervising and disciplining children as well as encouraging modesty, diligence, and obedience.[9] Schools, which became more public and strictly run in colonial America, grew to be an ally for parents in the battle to create ideal children and, in the long term, God-fearing and law-abiding adults.

Although a sense of childhood was firmly in place by 1700, it also should be noted that harsh methods of social control for children were still used and, in fact, strongly encouraged. Physical beatings were deemed a necessary component of effective discipline, and various pieces of evidence suggest "that by present standards, a large percentage of children born before the 1700s could be considered battered children."[10] The belief in the value of harsh physical punishments also can be seen in one of the first pieces of legislation directed at young people, which was enacted in Massachusetts in 1646.[11] This "stubborn child law" focused on incorrigibility and provided that if any son age 16 or older failed to obey his parents, he should be brought before the magistrates.

The law in Massachusetts was written directly at young males, presumably because daughters were thought to be less headstrong, and it illustrates how throughout history, young males have been known or thought to exhibit more problematic behavior than females.[12] If the son was found to be stubborn or rebellious and not able to obey his parents, the prescribed penalty was death. Although it appears that the sentence was never actually carried out, the law emphasizes harsh punishment with no hint of more modern ideas about prevention and rehabilitation. Furthermore, the similarities between the theory and administration of this law and that of modern death penalty statutes are striking.[13] The law was seemingly based on a belief in general deterrence (that the threat of death would prevent incorrigibility), but it stipulated a penalty that was apparently never carried out. As with the modern death penalty, there was high prescribed severity but little certainty of punishment.

During the course of the 1700s, ideas about childhood and beliefs in the value of proper childrearing strengthened, as did norms and expectations about the behavior of children. Life in that century became dominated by three major social institutions: family, church, and community.[14] Families were given increasing responsibility for socializing children and instilling social control. The church was to oversee family practices as well as adult behavior and ensure that children were provided with care, supervision, and discipline. Children, in turn, were expected to be respectful and obedient. Finally, the larger community was to be a safety net of supervision and control. Schools and beliefs in the value of education became more ingrained and accepted as necessary components of childrearing.

Although the behavior of children received increasing attention during this time, there was no notion of delinquency, and crime committed by an individual of any age was essentially equated with sin. Human nature was still viewed as inherently evil; therefore, crime and sin were to be expected, and few differences were seen between the behavior of children and adults or between serious and minor offenses. However, the establishment of the concept of childhood did provide the idea that children could be shaped and formed into law-abiding adults. The focus, though, remained on harsh physical punishment and retribution, which was anticipated to produce strict obedience in children.

This belief in the value of harsh physical punishments corresponded in time with the establishment of the classical school of criminology, which proposed that humans are rational beings who will naturally seek to maximize pleasure and avoid pain.[15] Led by Cesare Beccaria in the mid-1700s, this school of thought emphasized a fair system of punishment that would deter both known and potential offenders from future criminal behavior. It was not until the early 1800s that strong distinctions began to be made between younger and older offenders and that other methods of sanctioning and correcting behavior began to be considered and used.

ADOLESCENCE AND THE CREATION OF DELINQUENCY

Prior to the 1800s, Americans generally relied on traditional common law that did not allow children younger than 7 years old to be tried and found guilty of serious crime.[16] Between the ages of 7 and 14, young people also basically were assumed to be innocent and unable to fully understand the nature of their sins. If judges or juries determined, however, that a youth did know right from wrong, a finding of guilt was possible and severe punishment could be imposed. Beyond the age of 14, individuals essentially were viewed as adults although exceptions were made, as in the death penalty component of the previously mentioned stubborn child law. By the early 1800s, though, several developments and events occurred that contributed to the eventual establishment of a separate system of juvenile justice.

First, authoritarian Puritan ideals were being increasingly challenged, and appropriate childhood behavior began to be viewed more as a product of love and affection rather than fear and submission.[17] Enlightened philosophy stressed a more optimistic view of human nature and human progress, and children in particular came to be seen as innately good and able to be obedient because they wanted to be that way. Family life remained of utmost importance, but strong emotional ties and positive interactions were to replace fierce confrontations and harsh punishment. Furthermore, the notion that crime and sin were synonymous began to be rejected, and criminal tendencies started to be traced to breakdowns in family functioning during early childhood.

Second, along with changing beliefs about childhood behavior and family interactions, an emerging idea of adolescence originated.[18] The previous concept of childhood gradually extended into the teenage years, and youths who had been viewed as adults came to be seen as more childlike. They tended to remain at home and be dependent on their parents for longer time periods, and they also were considered future adults who had not yet become set in their ways. This developing notion of adolescence meant that teenagers who broke the law might still be salvageable if appropriate actions were taken.

Third, urbanization and growing concerns about poverty contributed greatly to the development of delinquency as a concept.[19] Prior to the late 1700s, American and European societies were mostly rural and agricultural. By the early 1800s, most major cities had experienced rapid population growth that had been spurred by immigration and the promise of industrial jobs. In general, cities were highly unprepared for this dramatic expansion, and many people who moved to urban areas were unskilled and poor. Families were subjected to substandard living conditions, and poor and homeless children and adolescents began to be viewed as a serious problem on the streets. Concerns about juvenile crime committed by lower-class young people, combined with changing beliefs about childhood, adolescence, and the importance of proper nurturance and supervision, set the stage for special efforts to deal with delinquent children and youths. The use of the term "juvenile delinquency" can be traced to London in 1816; in New York City, the Society for the Reformation of Juvenile Delinquents was founded in 1819.[20] The new concept and organized movements to address delinquency spread rapidly. Although reformers emphasized environmental factors as producers of delinquents, delinquency itself generally was seen as a consequence of the poor being unable to provide their children with a proper moral upbringing. Delinquents, then, were not only children and youths who broke the law. By the 1820s, any poor young person who appeared to lack adequate parental supervision and guidance could be labeled a delinquent and identified for special attention.

THE CREATION OF JUVENILE INSTITUTIONS

Between 1780 and 1825, the population of New York City grew from about 12,000 to more than 166,000.[21] Other major cities, such as Boston, Philadelphia, and Chicago, also grew quickly, but not as early and fast as New York. Efforts to address juvenile delinquency in New York City were led by white, male Protestants who were both threatened by and concerned about urbanization, immigration, and poverty. "Pauperism" was specified as the key issue.[22] Paupers were poor people who were believed to be poor because of their own wicked, unruly, lazy, and violent ways. If they only were hard-working and honest, it was thought, they would not be poor. Also, children of paupers were of particular concern because of the perceived likelihood that they would grow up to be like their parents if something was not done to correct the situation. Pauper children and delinquents were essentially one and the same and became the focus of reformation efforts.

By the late 1700s, there was a growing belief that confinement was a more effective punishment than previously used harsh physical sanctions.[23] In addition to providing punishment, confinement offered the potential for rehabilitation and better maintenance of social order. Short-term jails were converted to longer-term prisons, which housed a wide variety of both juvenile delinquents and adult criminals. In the early 1820s, concerns about pauperism and delinquency merged with the strengthening belief in confinement as reformers suggested that poor children and minor juvenile offenders were being harmed by being placed in the company of adult criminals in prison. Recommendations emerged for separate facilities for juvenile delinquents that would focus on prevention and rehabilitation rather than punishment. In New York City, these efforts resulted in the opening of the New York House of Refuge in 1825;[24] within three years, Boston and Philadelphia quickly followed in opening their own facilities.[25]

The House of Refuge

Houses of refuge were intended to hold both young criminals and other children in need (that is, children of paupers). In many or most cases, youths in these facilities had broken no laws but were placed for their own good. The house of refuge was to substitute for inadequate parents in providing education, discipline, and an environment that stressed hard work and strong moral values. It should be noted that only children who presented some potential for change were to be sent to these institutions and more serious juvenile offenders remained in adult prisons.[26] In other words, an early form of juvenile transfer was in place, essentially based on amenability to treatment in houses of refuge. However, no separate system of juvenile justice existed at this time beyond the special reformatories for poor and delinquent children.

Because being sent to a house of refuge did not require a criminal conviction, and because of the supposed emphasis on prevention and rehabilitation, little or no attention was paid to due process rights of delinquent youths. Juveniles could be committed until their eighteenth or twenty-first birthdays in an effort to correct for inadequate parenting and build moral values in a highly structured environment. As a result of overcrowding, a "placing out" system also soon developed, whereby many youths were sent to work on farms in midwestern states. According to Thomas Bernard:

> The House of Refuge quickly became a shipping station for poor children who were thought to be in danger of growing up to be paupers. They would be removed from their families and would spend about a year in the House of Refuge learning good work habits. They then would be placed on trains headed west, where they would be indentured out for service until they reached 21.... Over 50,000 children were removed from New York City in this way.[27]

Legal Challenges

Perhaps not surprisingly, legal challenges arose in response to the practices of houses of refuge. In 1838, in the case of Mary Ann Crouse, the Pennsylvania Supreme Court upheld the state commitment of a juvenile to an institution without any requirement for due process rights.[28] Crouse's father had challenged his daughter's placement in the Philadelphia House of Refuge on the basis that there should be no punishment unless a crime has been committed. (She had not been charged with any offense.) The court, however, ruled that Mary Ann Crouse was being helped, not punished, by being placed in the facility, and the good intentions of the house of refuge were contrasted with the poor performance of Crouse's parents. Moreover, the court elaborated on the concept of *parens patriae*, a Latin phrase meaning "parent of the county" that originally was used in England in the 1500s.[29] At that time, English Chancery Courts used the doctrine of *parens patriae* to manage estates of orphaned children until they turned 21. The Pennsylvania Supreme Court extended the concept to poor children whose parents were still alive and, in doing so, asserted that due process rights were not required in these types of cases.

Following the *Crouse* case, houses of refuge continued to open and expand across the country. However, by the mid-1800s, they were no longer seen as a panacea or cure-all for the problem of juvenile delinquency.[30] Rather than providing nurturance and rehabilitation, most of these institutions were prison-like warehouses that experienced increasing levels of violence among staff and inmates. Corporal punishment became the dominant mode of treatment along with manual labor.[31] As the placing out system began to break down, more and more youths were released from overcrowded facilities in shorter amounts of time.[32] Rising criticisms contributed to various attempts at reform such as the implementation of smaller programs and rural cottage settings, but the custodial and often harsh character of juvenile institutions remained.[33] This set the stage for a large-scale social movement in the latter half of the 1800s that eventually culminated in a separate system of juvenile justice.

THE PROGRESSIVE MOVEMENT AND THE JUVENILE COURT

At the same time that houses of refuge were coming under increased scrutiny and losing their "idealized glow,"[34] the case of Daniel O'Connell was making its way to the Illinois Supreme Court. Similar to Mary Ann Crouse, Daniel O'Connell had not committed any illegal offense but was judged to be in need of proper supervision and care and in danger of growing up to be a pauper.[35] He therefore was committed to the Chicago House of Refuge, where he potentially could have remained until age 21. Also like Mary Ann Crouse, Daniel O'Connell's father challenged his son's confinement and sought to have him released. In contrast to the *Crouse* decision, however, in 1870 the Illinois Supreme Court sided with O'Connell and ordered that he be discharged from custody.

In its deliberations, the Illinois Supreme Court determined that O'Connell was being punished instead of helped by being placed in the facility, and the poor actual performance of the house of refuge was compared unfavorably with the good intentions of the youth's parents. The court also rejected the doctrine of *parens patriae* as a basis for dealing with youths in this manner. Under the circumstances, then, the court concluded that some basic due process rights were needed. So, despite very similar circumstances and case characteristics, the Illinois Supreme Court reached the opposite decision of that provided by the Pennsylvania

Supreme Court about 30 years earlier. Although the decision itself did not have an immediate and dramatic impact on juvenile justice,[36] it was a strong sign of the times and contributed to the efforts of reformers who were both concerned about the treatment provided to youths in correctional facilities and increasingly critical of the practice of adjudicating delinquency in adult criminal courts.

East Coast Child Savers

By the time of the case of Daniel O'Connell, groups of reformers collectively known as "child savers" were advocating and instituting new measures to address the problem of delinquency. On the East Coast, upper-class philanthropists, who were referred to as "charity workers," founded new societies in an attempt to save poor children from delinquent and criminal lifestyles.[37] These individuals tended to be more optimistic about the possibility of reforming youths, preferred family life and community-based services rather than institutions such as houses of refuge and other reform schools, and felt compelled to try to overcome the perceived negative effects of rapid urbanization. They also emphasized prevention and early intervention, and they objected to more reactive institutional practices that reached limited numbers of children and youths.

The efforts of the East Coast charity workers led to the creation of the Five Points Mission, the New York Juvenile Asylum, and the Children's Aid Society in the 1850s, and methods of working with poor children and their families in the home and community environment subsequently became preferred over institutionalization. Initially, the East Coast child savers were proponents of the same placing out system that originated in houses of refuge, whereby youths were removed from poverty-ridden urban areas and sent to live with foster families in the midwest.[38] However, because of due process concerns, undesirable and inadequate numbers of foster homes, and the involuntary and sometimes abusive nature of this practice, in the latter quarter of the nineteenth century family- and community-based services became popular and dominant.

Another important aspect of the East Coast child-saving movement represents the basis for the formal practice of probation as we know it today. In the early 1840s, a Boston shoemaker by the name of John Augustus began to provide bail and the promise to supervise men who had been charged with drunkenness.[39] He soon extended his services to young people (both males and females), providing them with clothing and shelter and assisting them with finding a job and complying with court requirements. Boston courts became increasingly supportive of this practice, and by the late 1860s, Massachusetts had a system in place that granted officers responsibility for supervising children who had come under the care of the state. After becoming a regular part of Massachusetts's approach to dealing with juvenile delinquency, the idea of probation in lieu of institutionalization spread to several other states, setting an important precedent for formal juvenile justice practices soon to be implemented across the United States.

Chicago Child Savers

In the late 1800s and early 1900s, a nationwide progressive movement occurred that was fueled by rapid urbanization, massive immigration, and the United States establishing itself as a worldwide power.[40] During the Progressive Era, social conditions became an increasingly important issue and target for change. Furthermore, those in positions of economic power began to fear "that the urban masses would destroy the world they had built."[41] These beliefs also corresponded with the rise of the positive school of criminology, which emphasized using scientific methods to test hypotheses about the causes of criminal behavior.[42] Led by Cesare Lombroso and others, this school of thought proposed that individual characteristics and social conditions, more so than free will and rational choice, influence behavior and can be identified through scientific inquiry.

In this context, skepticism arose about the effectiveness of informal attempts to alleviate miserable social conditions and reform delinquent and criminal individuals, and many began to suggest that the threat of social disorder required a more formal and scientific approach to maintaining an orderly society. Nowhere else was this progressive movement more evident than in Chicago at the turn of the century. As summarized by Thomas Bernard,

> No city grew as rapidly as Chicago did in the 1800s. A person who was born in Chicago in 1840 started life in a village of 5,000 people. By the time that person was 60 years old in 1900, Chicago was a gigantic metropolis of 1,500,000. This growth was fueled by wave upon wave of immigrants. In 1890, 70% of the people who lived in Chicago were born

in foreign countries. Most of the rest were first-generation Americans whose parents were born abroad.[43]

In this context, Chicago faced special difficulties associated with rises in juvenile delinquency. Its house of refuge and some other facilities had been destroyed by fire in 1871 and, based on the ruling by the Illinois Supreme Court in the case of Daniel O'Connell, criminal courts essentially lost jurisdiction over children who had been deemed at risk but had not committed a felony. Those remaining under court jurisdiction often were held in jail with adult inmates and were processed in criminal court, where they could be subjected to prison sentences. In fact, by 1898, "575 boys were in the county jail and 1,983 [were] in the city prison."[44]

Progressive reformers in Chicago saw several problems with this situation. First, it was perceived that little was being done with nondelinquent youths and other minor offenders who were believed to be in need of proper supervision and guidance. Second, adjudicating youths in criminal court and placing them in adult correctional facilities was a major concern. Conditions in jails and prisons were deplorable, particularly for children, and the potential for abuse was high. This led judges to release many youths charged with serious crime without any further sentence being imposed. In the late 1800s, the Chicago Child Savers argued that doing little or nothing with many at-risk and delinquent youths while at the same time subjecting other young offenders to the abuse and influence of adult inmates in substandard jails and prisons was a bad combination in need of attention. The main problem was to find a way to formally treat at-risk and delinquent youths outside the bounds of the adult criminal system. This issue was addressed most vigorously by the Chicago Women's Club.[45]

Whereas houses of refuge and most other early efforts directed at juvenile delinquency greatly involved the work of men, the first official juvenile court was greatly the result of the work of women. These women were relatively conservative and primarily were the wives and daughters of prominent politicians and businessmen in Chicago.[46] They also tended to be white, Anglo-Saxon, Protestant, and affluent, and they generally sought a way to provide public service while maintaining the traditional women's role with regard to family, children, and taking care of the home. Directing their efforts toward poor children in need allowed these women to become involved in politics. In 1895, the Chicago Women's Club drafted a bill to create a separate juvenile court and probation staff.[47] Shortly thereafter, these women were supported by the Illinois Conference of Charities and the Chicago Bar Association,[48] and in 1899 the Illinois Juvenile Court Act was passed by the state legislature.

This legislation provided the newly created juvenile court with broad jurisdiction for all children younger than age 16 (later raised to 17 for boys and 18 for girls) who were perceived to be in need of supervision and guidance.[49] This included both delinquent children who had broken the law or exhibited other delinquent tendencies, such as incorrigibility or truancy, and dependent or neglected children who were not receiving proper parental care or guardianship. Essentially, the law was written so broadly that virtually any poor child could be brought under the jurisdiction of the juvenile court. The doctrine of *parens patriae* again was used to form the foundation of this system because the new juvenile court was to act as a chancery court for children in need rather than a criminal court for adult law violators.[50] The establishment of a separate court system for juveniles allowed for the earlier Illinois Supreme Court decision to be bypassed while at the same time facilitating the process of serving the perceived "best interests" of delinquent, dependent, and neglected children and youths.

In distinguishing itself from adult criminal court, the juvenile court was to emphasize and employ a unique philosophy and procedure.[51] First, the juvenile court embraced the modern concept of childhood that had been emerging during the course of several centuries and stressed the notion that children should be treated differently than adults. Second, juvenile court hearings were to be of an informal nature, involving only a judge, a child, his or her parents, and a probation officer. Due process rights were given little attention, with the rationale that determining guilt and providing punishment was much less a concern than identifying the child's needs and administering appropriate treatment and rehabilitative measures. Third, in carrying out its function, the juvenile court was to use a distinct language that, in contrast to the terms used in criminal court, denoted "a sense of problems, needs, concern, helping, and caring."[52] Rather than being indicted, for example, youths were petitioned to juvenile court, where they were subject to adjudication and disposition rather than trial and sentencing. Finally, the juvenile court sought to prioritize the use of probation in lieu of incarceration, and the court was to serve as a central referral unit for a variety of social service organizations and agencies. In general, this enabled coercive treatment to be provided to "salvageable" children and youths.

THE SPREAD OF JUVENILE COURTS

Drawing on Chicago's model, the establishment of juvenile courts spread rapidly throughout the United States. By 1912, 22 states had passed juvenile court laws, and by 1925, all but two states had done so.[53] In 1945, Wyoming became the last state to establish a juvenile court.[54] Although no uniform juvenile justice system was implemented, progressive reformers celebrated the creation of the juvenile court as a major achievement, and a great sense of optimism existed with regard to the court's potential for preventing and reducing juvenile delinquency. Moreover, the juvenile court provided a vehicle for further middle-class control over children of the poor but did so in a more community-based environment that provided relief from the problems of institutional crowding and substandard conditions. Still, many youths continued to be placed in secure correctional facilities for indefinite time periods as juvenile court judges typically imposed indeterminate sentences that allowed for release only when rehabilitation had been completed.

Pennsylvania was one of a large number of states that quickly followed Illinois in establishing its own juvenile court. In 1905, a decision by the Pennsylvania Supreme Court in the case of Frank Fisher reflected the optimistic way in which juvenile courts were viewed in the early 1900s.[55] Fisher was a 14-year-old boy who had been charged with but not convicted of larceny in Philadelphia, and he was placed in an institution where he could have been held until age 21. Similar to the earlier cases of Mary Ann Crouse and Daniel O'Connell, Fisher's father challenged his son's confinement on the basis that the punishment was disproportionate to the seriousness of the offense, for which no determination of guilt had occurred. As it did in the Crouse case 60 years earlier, the Pennsylvania Supreme Court rejected the arguments of Fisher's father and sided with the newly created juvenile court.

In deciding this case, the Pennsylvania Supreme Court returned to the same basic issues that were central to both the *Crouse* and *O'Connell* rulings. The court asserted that the juvenile was being helped, not punished, by the actions of the juvenile court, and the good intentions of the state outweighed the perceived poor performance of Fisher's parents.

Also, because of the special status and purpose of the juvenile court, the doctrine of *parens patriae* was deemed a legal foundation on which the juvenile court could operate. Finally, because of the child-saving nature of the juvenile court, the Pennsylvania Supreme Court specifically stated that there was no need for basic due process protections.[56]

Consistent with the views revealed in the Fisher case, juvenile courts generally "enjoyed widespread support for about two-thirds of the twentieth century."[57] Although various critics questioned the continued placement of children in jails and other correctional facilities for often-lengthy periods of time and issues arose surrounding the effectiveness of juvenile court treatment and abuses of power by the court, popular opinion held that the desirable aspects of a separate system of juvenile justice outweighed the undesirable consequences. During the past 40 years, however, much dissatisfaction and debate has arisen concerning the juvenile court's philosophy, structure, and procedures.[58] The changes that have resulted from these more contemporary attacks will be discussed shortly.

SUMMARY AND CONCLUSIONS

We have seen that the concepts of childhood, adolescence, and delinquency took several centuries to develop and evolve, dating back to the Middle Ages. In America, as community and family life became more child centered in the 1700s, assertions began to be made that children should receive special consideration and treatment. Still, until well into the 1800s, children accused and convicted of crimes were subjected to the same (often harsh) sanctions as those given to adult criminals. In other words, although some allowances were made for age and criminal culpability, juvenile offenders generally were treated the same as adults. This historical point should not be lost in modern discussions of transferring juveniles to the adult criminal justice system.

In the early 1800s, with the concept of childhood firmly in place and the notion of adolescence emerging, further concerns arose regarding the supervision and guidance of poor children in expanding urban areas as well as the placement of young offenders in jails and prisons with adult inmates. This, again, seems like an important time period to consider in contemporary debates concerning juvenile waiver to adult court. By the mid-1820s, increasing concerns led to the establishment of houses of refuge, which were expected to handle the problem of juvenile delinquency.

Houses of refuge and subsequent reform schools separated at-risk and delinquent youths from adult criminals, and the institutions were anticipated to provide a structured environment, treatment and rehabilitative services, and the eventual return to the community of law-abiding young citizens. *Parens patriae* was used as the fundamental basis for this approach, justifying state intervention into family life.

During the course of the 1800s, houses of refuge and other related responses to delinquency came to been seen as inadequate and even abusive, and legal decisions further dismantled the practice of confining non-delinquents and minor youthful offenders through adult court system processing. Progressive reformers focused their efforts on the placement of more serious delinquents in adult jails and prisons while little was being done with at-risk youths. By the late 1800s, growing understanding of child development contributed to adolescence being established as a new stage of preadulthood, and women became involved prominently in organized child-saving efforts. These issues and developments culminated in the creation of the first juvenile court in Cook County, Illinois, in 1899. The rest of the nation quickly followed in embracing a separate system of juvenile justice, with *parens patriae* again serving as the legal foundation. For the next 60 years, juvenile courts generally continued to operate using an optimistic philosophy of rehabilitation and individualized justice.

It is noteworthy that "juvenile courts did not develop in any highly specific fashion after 1899."[59] In general, juvenile courts operated with varying degrees of separation from criminal courts, and in many cases juvenile and criminal courts shared jurisdiction for certain youthful offenders. Juveniles who committed serious offenses and others who no longer were deemed to be "salvageable" could be sent to adult criminal court.[60] After a time, juvenile courts sought to enhance their authority by asserting that the determination as to whether a juvenile case should be moved to adult court should be made within the juvenile court. In this context, waiving a case to adult court became a decision based on whether a youth was beyond the rehabilitative capabilities of the juvenile system. We will now turn our attention to how this practice of juvenile transfer grew and evolved during the 1900s.

CHAPTER 3

Transformation to Criminal

In Chapter 1, the case of Nathaniel Abraham was introduced. In 1997, when he was 11 years old, Nathaniel shot and killed Ronnie Green. Subsequently, as possibly the youngest offender in American history to face murder charges as an adult,[1] Nathaniel was tried under a new law that enabled Michigan prosecutors to charge youths younger than 14 as adults for certain serious and violent crimes.[2] In other words, based on a prosecutor's decision, Nathaniel's case bypassed traditional juvenile court proceedings, and he was put on trial as an adult murder defendant. This case exemplifies the modern trend toward transforming many serious and violent youthful offenders into adult criminals with little or no input from the juvenile court.

The reduced or eliminated involvement of the juvenile court in the determination of which "hard" cases should be transferred to adult court usually is viewed as a contemporary reform, but it actually can be traced to the origins of juvenile waiver in the early twentieth century. The practice of transferring certain youths to adult criminal court developed and evolved following the juvenile court's inception and during the course of the 1900s, but the modern transfer movement that has taken place over the past 15 years is of particular concern. As a model, changes in juvenile justice philosophy and transfer practices in Pennsylvania in the mid-1990s illustrate the ways in which most states have revised their approach to dealing with serious and violent youthful offenders in recent times.

ORIGINS OF JUVENILE TRANSFER

As discussed in Chapter 2, early juvenile courts emphasized an informal and protective environment, resting on a philosophy of rehabilitation and individualized justice. Juvenile court actions were designed to determine if a child was in need of care and what should be done to prevent a future life of crime. This orientation is evident in the following description of early juvenile court procedures in Boston:

> The sheltered location of the room, the absence of decoration, the dispensing with attendants and the exclusion of outsiders give the simplicity that is necessary to gain the undivided attention of the child, and give the quiet which is indispensable for hearing clearly what the child says and speaking to him in the calmest tone.... The child does not stand in front of the desk, because that would prevent the judge from seeing the whole of him, and the way the child stands and even the condition of his shoes are often useful aids to a proper diagnosis of the case. The child stands at the end of the platform where the judge can see him from top to toe, and the judge sits near the end, so he is close to the child and can reassure him if necessary by a friendly hand on the shoulder.[3]

In this setting, punishment was not viewed as a central goal. Delinquency was seen as an illness brought on by urbanization, industrialization, poverty, parental neglect, and other social diseases.[4] This perspective corresponded well with changing ideological assumptions in the field of criminology. In the latter half of the nineteenth century, positivism challenged the classical school belief that crime was a product of free will. The positive school emphasized determinism, or the need to identify causal variables that produce crime and delinquency. Thus, positive criminology combined with the progressive movement to produce a "rehabilitative ideal," whereby the juvenile court was to be given the tools and strategies necessary to effect change in the behavior of young people.

Theoretically, the juvenile court's proceedings were designed to identify the underlying causes of youthful misbehavior and provide the treatment necessary to prevent more serious criminal behavior from happening in the future. However, almost immediately following the creation of the juvenile court, debates arose about which children belonged within its jurisdiction:

> In Chicago, for example, ... the number of delinquency cases overwhelmed the nation's first juvenile court. The judge and chief probation officer had to find ways to control an overwhelming caseload for practical as well as political reasons. They tried to keep younger children out of court because their cases clogged the court's calendar and did not appear serious enough to merit a judge's attention. Less serious cases also diverted the court's attention from recidivists, whose lack of amenability to reform threatened the court's legitimacy.[5]

In addition to the practice of diverting younger offenders from juvenile court, early juvenile court judges also were given the discretion to transfer more serious delinquents to adult criminal court:

> Legislation in many states permitted juvenile court judges to transfer any given case to an adult court, an allowance that they occasionally took advantage of when the charge was especially serious. The Cook County juvenile court, for example, asked grand juries to weigh the merits of a regular indictment in about fifteen cases a year—a figure which represented no more than one percent of its cases but did include the most notorious. Typically these boys were older (sixteen, not twelve) and were arrested for "deeds of violence, daring holdups, carrying guns, thefts of considerable amounts, and rape." These transfers probably muted criticisms of the courts for coddling the criminal.[6]

Thus, the notion of treating serious and violent juvenile offenders as adults is not a new development. Many of the considerations pertaining to this practice also seem consistent across time. It is interesting that from the outset, juvenile courts appeared to wash their hands of youths who were perhaps the most in need of help. In fact, this was a part of the process of early juvenile courts successfully establishing themselves by defining which children and youths they could best serve. Early juvenile court judges feared that laws establishing juvenile courts would be struck down as unconstitutional.[7] Therefore, in addition to the formal waiver proceedings mentioned above, juvenile judges did not always assert the original and exclusive jurisdiction provided to them by law. This allowed for an informal system of transfer to develop, whereby prosecutors' decisions to handle cases of serious and violent adolescent offenders in adult criminal courts were not challenged. Cases of older youthful recidivists, particularly those who committed crimes while on probation, also typically were transferred to adult court based on a passive response by the juvenile court.

Although juvenile court laws and transfer practices varied from state to state, overcrowded caseloads, issues of constitutionality, and concerns about placing more serious and violent youthful offenders in the company of other children in institutions continued to influence the use of active and passive juvenile transfer throughout the first quarter of the twentieth century. At the same time, critics were beginning to question the use of this practice. Because of the informal nature of the juvenile court and the lack of any uniform structure, transfer proceedings and the characteristics of transferred youths exhibited much diversity from state to state and from rural to urban courts. Although appellate court decisions tended to uphold the use of early transfer methods, the efforts of various progressive child advocates prompted most states not only to raise the maximum age of juvenile court jurisdiction to age 18 but also to legislatively exclude certain crimes (typically murder) from the jurisdiction of juvenile court.

JUVENILE JUSTICE PHILOSOPHY AND THE EVOLUTION OF TRANSFER

During the past century, American juvenile courts generally have asserted, "Children are developmentally different from adults; they are developing emotionally and cognitively; they are impressionable; and they have different levels of understanding than adults."[8] This underlying belief has been used to support three philosophical principles that are central to juvenile justice administration.[9] First, children and adolescents are assumed to have diminished capacity to fully appreciate or control their actions; this generally reduces their responsibility or culpability for illegal acts. Second, because of their diminished capacity, it is assumed that sanctions provided to juvenile offenders should not only be in proportion to the offense committed but these youths also should not receive the "full measure of punishment" provided to adult criminals. Third, the notion of "room to reform" has been used in an effort to reduce the permanent costs of adolescent mistakes and enable a more successful transition to adulthood with life chances intact.

These philosophical underpinnings have formed the basis for distinguishing between juvenile courts and adult criminal courts. However, they also have been used from time to time by those who have criticized the juvenile court as being too lenient or "soft on crime." For example, "in the 1920s and 1930s, the charge that juvenile courts coddled criminals was a much greater threat to the legitimacy of these courts than scattered procedural critiques by academics and judges."[10] In turn, it was at this time that advocates of the juvenile court strongly promoted the practice of judicial waiver as a way to counteract criticisms of the court being too soft on crime. Although prosecutors continued to file charges in adult criminal court against many juvenile murder defendants and appellate courts generally upheld this practice, by the late 1930s supporters of juvenile justice had established that judicial waiver was an essential part of juvenile justice that could be used to send certain appropriate cases to the adult criminal system.

Embracing the judicial waiver of juvenile court jurisdiction for more serious and violent youthful offenders served as an extension of the practice first used by early juvenile court judges. However, whereas early juvenile court judges actively or passively waived a relatively small number of youths (mainly to ensure the continued existence of the juvenile court and to protect other children in reform schools), in the late 1930s the expanded practice of judicial waiver could be seen as a reflection of the growing belief that certain types of adolescent offenders were not amenable to the rehabilitative efforts of the juvenile court. In other words, "the threat to public safety, no longer the safety of children in reform schools, had become the justification for waiver."[11]

Juvenile Court Criticisms

Although there were occasional constitutional debates and sporadic criticisms of the juvenile court following its creation, the related philosophy and procedures largely went unchallenged until after the middle of the twentieth century.[12] In the 1950s and 1960s, critics became increasingly vocal about the deficiencies of the juvenile system. The first round of criticisms focused on the lack of procedural safeguards granted to youthful offenders in juvenile court.[13] The informality of court hearings and the broad discretionary power granted to juvenile justice officials specifically were attacked. The concern for due process rights grew as it became apparent that the juvenile system often exhibited the same concern for punishment and incapacitation as the adult criminal system:

> Critics began to question the major assumptions underlying the jurisprudence of the juvenile court, and to recognize the *de facto* punitive characteristics of the juvenile court's sanctions. A concern for procedural protections in juvenile court decision processes grew in part as it became more apparent that in practice the functions of the juvenile justice system closely resembled those of the criminal justice system—punishment, deterrence, and incapacitation of persons who violated the criminal law. To the extent that the aims of the juvenile justice system increasingly approximated those of the criminal justice system, critics argued that juvenile offenders should be accorded the procedural safeguards granted to adults.[14]

Attention given to the inadequacies of juvenile court proceedings also was prompted by concerns about the broad discretionary powers provided to juvenile officials to commit and release youths as well as worries about potential negative labeling effects inherent in many delinquency proceedings.[15] Criticisms and efforts directed at these perceived problems eventually led to the "due process revolution" of the late 1960s and early 1970s, when several U.S. Supreme Court decisions established that juveniles could not be totally cut off from fundamental constitutional rights under the guise of "individualized justice."[16] Because of the discretionary nature of juvenile waiver practices at this time and the fact that a decision to transfer resulted in the identification of a youth as a criminal who would be processed in the adult criminal justice system, it is perhaps not surprising that transfer to adult court would be the first issue in juvenile justice addressed by America's highest court.

Supreme Court Cases

In 1966, in the landmark case of *Kent v. United States*, the U.S. Supreme Court examined the transfer of 16-year-old Morris Kent Jr. by the District of Columbia's juvenile court.[17] This case involved charges of housebreaking, robbery, and rape, and the District's criminal code provided for transfer to adult court only after a full investigation had taken place. However, in being waived to adult court, Morris was denied a formal hearing, and his attorney had no opportunity to review the existing juvenile file. Based on the circumstances of this case, the Court ruled that prior to being transferred to adult criminal court by a juvenile court judge, a youth has the right to a formal hearing regarding the waiver criteria and a right to counsel at this hearing. The Court also noted that the benefits and protections supposedly extended to youths in juvenile court do not negate the need for certain due process rights:

> While there can be no doubt of the original laudable purpose of juvenile courts, studies and critiques in recent years raise serious questions as to whether actual performance measures well enough against theoretical purpose to make tolerable the immunity of the process from the reach of constitutional guaranties applicable to adults. There is much evidence that some juvenile courts, including that of the District of Columbia, lack the personnel, facilities and techniques to perform adequately as representatives of the State in a *parens patriae* capacity. There is evidence, in fact, that there may be grounds for concern that the child receives the worst of both worlds: that he gets neither the protections accorded to adults nor the solicitous care and regenerative treatment postulated for children.[18]

The case of Morris Kent was significant to the practice of juvenile transfer in three main ways.[19] First, an appendix of "determinative factors" was created by the Supreme Court justices that provided broad guidelines to be considered in potential transfer cases. These guidelines subsequently were adopted into juvenile laws by most state legislatures.[20] Second, the *Kent* decision came at a time when faith in the rehabilitative ideal of the juvenile court was being questioned, and "just deserts" was being asserted by reformers as a new philosophy. In general, use of more formal waiver mechanisms reflected a growing desire for greater emphasis on fair and consistent punishment in response to illegal behavior, which became known as just deserts. Third, this case generated a great deal of attention to the transfer of juveniles to adult court, and researchers began to study this process and its consequences in much more detail.

The following year, the case of Gerald Gault further established that juveniles who face institutional confinement require the procedural safeguards of advanced notice of charges, legal representation, the opportunity to confront and cross-examine witnesses, and the privilege against self-incrimination.[21] This case involved a 15-year-old boy who had been arrested for making an "obscene" telephone call to a female neighbor and subsequently was placed in a state industrial school for up to his twenty-first birthday. The offense allegedly involved the following questions: "Do you give any?" "Are your cherries ripe today?" and "Do you have big bombers?"[22] No record was kept of the adjudication hearing, and the victim did not appear.

In extending several more due process rights to juveniles, the Supreme Court asserted in *Gault* that the benefits of the juvenile court and the juvenile court's unique procedures for processing youths separately from adults should be available without any reduction in the law's protection. The Court also directed strong words at juvenile courts that fail to recognize basic due process rights: "It would be extraordinary if our Constitution did not require the procedural regularity and the exercise of care implied in the phrase 'due process.' Under our Constitution, the condition of being a boy does not justify a kangaroo court."[23] In the 1970s, the Supreme Court continued to address the issue of due process protections for juveniles. With the *In re Winship* decision, the Court asserted that in delinquency proceedings, the standard of proof required is "beyond a reasonable doubt" rather than "by preponderance of the evidence."[24] In *Breed v. Jones*, the Court returned to the issue of juvenile transfer and found that the protections of the double jeopardy clause of the Fifth Amendment require juvenile courts to make a decision to waive jurisdiction to criminal court prior to any determination of guilt.[25] Although the Supreme Court stopped short of extending to juveniles all the procedural safeguards given to adults (for example, right to a jury trial, right to bail),[26] by the mid-1970s the juvenile court had been moved away from its original progressive orientation and toward a more procedurally formal system that emphasized substantive justice.

Rehabilitation, Crime, and Punishment

While initial criticisms of the juvenile court focused on constitutional rights and procedural fairness, "the second wave of criticisms and reforms that emerged in the mid-1970s into the 1980s was specifically directed at changing the goals and structure of the system."[27] Here, critics focused primarily on two areas: the perceived ineffectiveness of rehabilitation programs and rapidly rising crime rates. In a short period of time, concerns about these two factors would lead to rather dramatic changes in juvenile justice philosophy and practice.

In the 1970s, several influential reviews of research on correctional rehabilitation programs were conducted in an effort to identify those programs that were effective in reducing future offending.[28] In general, the findings of these studies seemed to suggest that "nothing works." Reservation about the potential for rehabilitation conflicted strongly with the juvenile court's traditional emphasis on treatment and individualized care. Furthermore, court dispositions that removed youths from the community and placed them in a secure facility were increasingly seen as inherently punitive rather than rehabilitative. Therefore, questioning of the procedural fairness of juvenile court operations was followed by criticisms of the court's effectiveness in rehabilitating youths.

In addition to the apparent inability of the juvenile system to provide effective rehabilitative services, crimes committed by young people increased rapidly from the mid-1960s through the mid-1970s, and "crime in the streets" soon became a dominant public and political concern.[29] By the late 1970s and early 1980s, a popular view emerged that juvenile courts were too lenient, particularly with serious and violent offenders. Assertions were made that the juvenile system was unable to ensure public safety, and a number of commentators argued that the juvenile court essentially had outlived its usefulness.[30]

Combined with earlier constitutional challenges, concerns over the efficacy of rehabilitation and rising youth crime encouraged a thorough reexamination of the juvenile court's structure and philosophy. Similar to changes in ideology that occurred previously in the adult criminal system, the overall response was a rapid shift toward a more punitive juvenile system that emphasized accountability, deterrence, and incapacitation.[31] Commitment to the rehabilitative ideal gave way to a concentration on ensuring just desserts, and a get-tough-on-crime approach was supported by politicians at all levels of government.[32] Jurisdiction after jurisdiction made modifications to their juvenile codes. Popular strategies included facilitating the transfer of youths to adult court, incorporating the goals of accountability and public safety into juvenile codes, and using determinate and mandatory sentencing in juvenile courts. It was hoped that these changes would be an effective response to the increasing public concern about juvenile crime.

The Youth Violence Epidemic

Interestingly, calls for abolishing the juvenile court and corresponding juvenile justice reforms in the early to mid-1980s came at a time when juvenile crime, including serious and violent offending, had stabilized and even declined for a period of several years. In fact, from the mid-1970s to the mid-1980s, official measures of virtually all forms of delinquent behavior revealed either very little fluctuation or decreasing trends.[33] However, by the middle to late 1980s, a change in the levels of youth violence emerged that soon had a dramatic impact on juvenile justice in America, specifically with regard to the transfer of serious and violent youthful offenders to adult criminal court.

As mentioned earlier, from the mid-1980s through the mid-1990s, violent juvenile crime arrest rates surged dramatically. While juvenile arrest rates for robbery and aggravated assault exhibited rapid growth, the surge in youth homicide rates was particularly disturbing. Not only did the juvenile murder arrest rate rise at a much faster pace than that of adults but for older youths the increase was more than 100%.[34] Furthermore, this increase in juvenile homicide rates corresponded with the accumulation of guns among young people.[35] Juvenile arrest rates for weapons law violations also climbed steadily, with the greatest upturn occurring after 1987. Not surprisingly, juvenile gun homicides rose dramatically while homicides involving other weapons remained steady.

Although a number of explanations had been put forth for the modern youth violence epidemic,[36] policymakers appeared to be influenced most by public worries surrounding both the high levels of juvenile violent offending in the early to mid-1990s and projected increases for the future. Knowledge about a growing juvenile population combined with fears that the new generation of violent youthful offenders was particularly vicious and bankrupt of moral values created a perceived need to "do something" about violent juvenile crime. Sensational predictions that juvenile violent crime rates would continue to increase and that juvenile offending would become even more heinous and deadly greatly accelerated efforts to "get tough" and "crackdown" on juvenile crime that originated in the early 1980s.

THE MODERN TRANSFER MOVEMENT

By the mid-1990s, a variety of juvenile justice reforms had been instituted across virtually the entire United States in an attempt to deal with the epidemic of youth violence.[37] In general, laws were passed that sought to deemphasize traditional juvenile court confidentiality concerns while increasing information sharing, expand juvenile court sentencing options and authority while stressing public safety and offender accountability, and increase the visibility and participation of victims and victim organizations in the juvenile justice process. The most popular and politically touted reform, though, was in the area of jurisdictional authority as all but 10 states adopted or modified laws between 1992 and 1995 that were intended to ease the process of transferring juveniles to adult criminal court. Several of the remaining states did so shortly thereafter.[38]

The trend toward greater use of expanded waiver laws can be traced to the rising concerns about juvenile crime and juvenile justice in the 1970s and early 1980s. During that time, about half of all state legislatures amended their juvenile codes to simplify or expedite the transfer of juveniles to adult court.[39] During the 1990s, efforts to facilitate juvenile waiver to the adult criminal justice system accelerated, and various new practices and procedures were added to those that already had been in existence for quite some time.

To begin, state legal codes exhibit wide variation in the age limitations placed on juvenile court jurisdiction. Minimum age restrictions for juvenile court jurisdiction often are not stipulated in state codes, which means that individual courts can either develop their own policies or rely on the common-law notion that no person can be held criminally responsible for his or her actions until the age of 7.[40] Maximum ages for original juvenile court jurisdiction range from 15 to 17 years of age, with 37 states and the District of Columbia using 17 as the upper age limit (that is, in these states, 18-year-old juveniles are considered adults). States also vary in the maximum age at which the juvenile court can retain control beyond the original oldest age of jurisdiction. Most states can retain control until the age of 21, or even higher (for example, delinquent youths in California, Montana, Oregon, and Wisconsin can remain under juvenile court jurisdiction for dispositional purposes up to age 25).

Regardless of their varying age limitations for juvenile court jurisdiction, today all states do have provisions that allow juveniles to be tried in adult court.[41] There is further state variation in the youngest age at which juveniles can be transferred, however. Many states have no minimum age limit (there is no exclusive juvenile court jurisdiction) while the lower limit for transfer in other states ranges from ages 10 to 15. In general, state transfer laws identify categories or characteristics (including age) of youthful offenders who may, or in some cases must, be sent to the adult criminal justice system. There are three primary mechanisms for juvenile transfer: judicial waiver, prosecutorial waiver, and legislative waiver.[42] Most states have some combination of these three procedures in place. Furthermore, during the past decade, several strategies have been implemented to both refine these basic methods and better regulate their use.

Judicial Waiver

Historically, transferring juveniles to adult criminal court has been accomplished most often through discretionary judicial waiver, whereby a juvenile court judge is granted the authority to make the key decision in the transfer process.[43] Currently, 46 states and the District of Columbia have judicial waiver provisions.[44] Under this method, a case against a young offender originates in juvenile court, and a juvenile court judge must make the decision to send the case to adult court. A judge's decision to waive a case normally requires a determination that the youth is no longer amenable to the treatment offered in the juvenile system based on such factors as age, offense seriousness, prior record, and public safety. This assessment reflects the individualized nature of dispositions that is characteristic of traditional juvenile courts. From the early to mid-1990s, about one third of all states sought to enhance their traditional judicial waiver practices by adding eligible crimes, lowering minimum age requirements, and/or adjusting prior record provisions.[45]

The practice of judicial waiver was addressed by the U.S. Supreme Court in *Kent v. United States* and in *Breed v. Jones*. Although these two cases established a procedural framework for judges to use in making waiver decisions, they by no means eliminated judicial discretion from the process.[46] In *Kent*, the majority opinion set forth several factors that a judge might consider in making a decision to transfer, but vague phrases such as "amenability to treatment," "best interests of the public," and "dangerousness" remain a central feature of judicial waiver laws.[47] This leads to the argument that judicial waiver provides judges with broad, standardless discretion, which allows inequities and disparities to occur.[48] In contrast, supporters of this method contend that individualized transfer procedures provide the flexibility necessary for sound decision-making to take place.[49]

Although discretionary judicial waiver remains the most common form of juvenile transfer law, two contemporary modifications to this practice have sought to change the nature of judicial waiver proceedings and reduce the juvenile court judge's discretion. In ordinary judicial waiver hearings, the prosecution bears the burden of proof to convince the juvenile judge that transfer to adult court is the most appropriate outcome.[50] Under presumptive judicial waiver laws, though, the burden of proof is shifted to the defense to show that the case should remain in juvenile court. Fourteen states and the District of Columbia currently have presumptive waiver laws, which designate certain categories of cases (usually based on age of the offender, offense seriousness, and prior record) that initially are presumed to be appropriate for waiver.[51] Essentially, these statutes "tip the balance in favor of the prosecution."[52]

Mandatory waiver laws far exceed presumptive waiver provisions by requiring juvenile courts to transfer certain cases to adult court for prosecution. The statutes of 15 states provide for mandatory waiver, again typically in cases involving certain combinations of offender age, offense seriousness, and prior record.[53] Although proceedings are initiated in juvenile court, the role of the judge is to confirm that the statutory requirements for mandatory waiver are met and then send the case to adult criminal court. Mandatory waiver provisions tend to be "quite narrow in the list of offenses reached and in the number of cases that fall within their scope. But they are important because they reflect legislative willingness to eliminate juvenile court discretion in the waiver system."[54]

Prosecutorial Waiver

Sometimes referred to as concurrent jurisdiction or direct file, prosecutorial waiver allows a prosecutor to file charges in either juvenile or adult court. This method often is limited to some combination of specific offenses (for example, violent or felony crimes), juveniles of a certain age, and those with prior adjudications in juvenile court. Prosecutorial waiver currently is used in 14 states and the District of Columbia,[55] and it is probably the most controversial method of transfer because of the wide discretion often granted to a typically "crime control-oriented" court official.[56] Moreover, as summarized by Barry Feld, "unlike a judge, who has the benefit of judicial waiver hearings ... where clinicians and court services personnel can provide information about a youth's maturity, sophistication, or amenability to treatment based on clinical evaluations, social service reports, interviews, and the like, prosecutors typically lack access to such personal information."[57]

Prosecutorial waiver is one way in which policymakers can seek to increase the number of juveniles transferred to adult court through enacting or expanding this practice by law, but relatively few states (less than 10) have done so in recent years.[58] Although prosecutors may enjoy the authority they are granted and use it to expedite the transfer process, critics contend that these officials can be influenced too easily by a perceived public demand for punishment, especially since there is no opportunity for any form of legal accountability or review.[59] Furthermore, the shift in discretion from juvenile court judges to prosecutors raises the question as to whether prosecutors can make better and more appropriate decisions (often with little information available) than would juvenile judges in waiver hearings that are guided by specified criteria.

Legislative Waiver

During the 1980s and 1990s, the literature reflected a growing opposition to both judicial and prosecutorial waiver, with calls to apply more objective criteria to the transfer process.[60] Perhaps in response to these attacks, increasing political support arose for a third method[61] of transfer that seeks to eliminate or reduce discretionary decision-making by judges and prosecutors. Legislative waiver, also known as statutory exclusion, places eligible youths into the adult criminal system at the time of arrest, thereby removing the initial discretionary power of juvenile court officials.[62]

Legislative waiver laws, which emphasize the use of offense criteria in determining the appropriate court of jurisdiction, are a strong indicator of the shift in juvenile justice from an individualized treatment philosophy to a more retributive orientation.[63] Supporters of this policy contend that, compared with the highly discretionary practices of judicial and prosecutorial waiver, there is improved uniformity in determining the correct court of jurisdiction. However, others point out that the process can be rigid and over-inclusive, as some excluded offenders may benefit from the treatment services offered in the juvenile system.[64] Furthermore, legislative waiver may simply switch discretionary decision-making from the juvenile court to the adult criminal court[65] because most states with legislative waiver provisions also allow cases to be "reverse waived" back to juvenile court for adjudication, disposition, or both.[66] In addition, prosecutors can reduce or dismiss charges, thereby eliminating criminal court jurisdiction.

Legislatures in 29 states currently have excluded certain offenses, offenders, or both from juvenile court jurisdiction.[67] The most commonly excluded crimes are murder and other violent crimes against persons (for example, in Arizona, California, Georgia, Louisiana, and Oregon), but youths charged with various felonies such as burglary who also have prior felony adjudications sometimes are targeted (for example, in Alaska, Florida, Idaho, Montana, Vermont, and Washington). In modern times, states that have made changes to the boundaries of their juvenile court jurisdictions most often did so through the use of statutory exclusion.[68] It is important to note that the most rapidly expanding method of transfer, legislative waiver, is also the one that has received the least amount of attention from the research community.[69]

Other Contemporary Waiver Strategies

In addition to the three basic forms of waiver discussed above, there have been several other contemporary strategies employed that pertain to the transfer of juveniles to adult court. For example, 25 states spread throughout the county currently allow juveniles in adult criminal court to petition for reverse waiver (also known as decertification) to juvenile court.[70] Reverse waiver laws most often coexist with legislative, prosecutorial, and mandatory judicial waiver, and they basically allow adult criminal courts to consider whether a case would be more appropriate for juvenile court processing. In most states, reverse waiver hearings are held prior to trial, but a few states (for example, California, Colorado, and Oregon) allow for decertification to occur following a determination of guilt (that is, the reverse waiver is for dispositional purposes only). In general, the adult court's reverse waiver decision is governed by similar "best interests" standards and considerations as those employed in juvenile court judicial waiver proceedings. Reverse waiver is therefore an example of a fail-safe mechanism that allows criminal court judges to make an individualized determination of a juvenile's suitability for adult court prosecution and sanctioning.[71]

A second modern approach to refining the practice of juvenile transfer involves the use of blended sentencing, which generally allows for a combination of juvenile and adult correctional sanctions to be imposed, regardless of court of jurisdiction.[72] More specifically, 15 states currently have juvenile blended sentencing schemes that enable juvenile courts to impose adult criminal sanctions on specified serious and violent offenders.[73] In most of these states (which include, Arkansas, Connecticut, Illinois, and Minnesota), the juvenile court can combine a juvenile disposition with a suspended criminal sentence, thereby allowing for the case potentially to be transferred to the adult system at a later date (that is, the suspended criminal sentence is used to encourage cooperation and compliance with treatment in the juvenile system). In addition to these inclusive juvenile blended sentence laws used in 11 states, four other states (Colorado, New Mexico, Rhode Island, and Texas) use either exclusive provisions that provide the juvenile court with the option to immediately impose criminal sanctions, which are contiguous sentences that carry over from the juvenile system to the adult system once a youth passes the maximum age of juvenile court jurisdiction.

In contrast to juvenile blended sentences, criminal blended sentencing laws enable adult court judges to impose sanctions on waived and convicted youths that normally would be available only in juvenile court.[74] A total of 17 states currently authorize adult courts to return transferred youths to the juvenile system for correctional purposes.[75] Ten states (for example, Kentucky, Massachusetts, Nebraska, and Wisconsin) have exclusive provisions that provide criminal courts with a choice between juvenile and adult sanctions, while the other seven (including, Idaho, Iowa, Michigan, and Virginia) employ inclusive laws that allow a combination of juvenile and adult sanctions to be imposed. While juvenile blended sentencing laws generally seek to strengthen the sentencing authority of juvenile courts, criminal blended sentencing represents an attempt to soften the effects of modern waiver laws based on the individual characteristics of the offense and offender (generally some combination of age, offense seriousness, and prior record).[76]

Finally, in 34 states, "once an adult/always an adult" provisions exist that force previously transferred juveniles to be prosecuted as adults if they subsequently are accused of new offenses.[77] Most of these states do require a conviction on the offense that triggered the original transfer to adult court for the subsequent waiver to occur automatically. There are exceptions to this rule, however. Some states (for example, California, Delaware, and Mississippi) do not require a conviction in the original case if certain circumstances exist (for example, the subsequent offense is a felony or a juvenile court previously determined the youth was no longer amenable to treatment in the juvenile system). Furthermore, although most states apply their once an adult/always an adult provisions to all subsequent offenses, several (Maryland, Michigan, Minnesota, and Texas) limit this practice only to subsequent felonies while others (Iowa and California) require a minimum offender age of 16 for the law to apply.

Transfer in Practice and Rationale

From 1998 through 2002, 31 states revised their laws governing the prosecution and sentencing of transferred youths.[78] This followed a five-year period during which nearly all states took action to toughen their juvenile codes, mainly through expanded waiver provisions. Despite this campaign of legislative activity and increased attention being given to transferred juveniles by researchers, relatively little information is available on the number of youths waived to adult court. In fact, "the [total] number of juvenile offenders currently being transferred to criminal courts in the United States is unknown."[79]

National estimates of the number of juvenile offenders who are judicially waived to adult court are available, but these figures represent only a small fraction of juveniles who are processed in the adult criminal system.[80] From the mid-1980s to the mid-1990s, during the decade long rise in youth violence, nationwide judicial waivers also increased substantially. As reported by Melissa Sickmund and colleagues, "between 1985 and 1994, the number of cases transferred annually to criminal court rose from 7,200 to 12,300 (71%)."[81] The number of judicial waivers grew larger than the corresponding increase in delinquency cases handled by juvenile courts; however, the percentage of petitioned delinquency cases that resulted in judicial waiver remained fairly even during this time period, at about 1%. Since 1994, as youth violence declined and states shifted to other transfer strategies, the use of judicial waiver has diminished. Recently published estimates indicate that in 1999 there were 7,500 judicially waived cases across the nation,[82] which is very similar to figures from the mid-1980s.

Several years ago, James Howell estimated that judicially waived cases represent only about 10% of all juveniles who are processed in the adult criminal system, as the other 90% end up in adult court through some other method.[83] Indeed, the percentage of juveniles in adult court who are waived there by a juvenile court judge actually might be in the lower single digits. Large numbers of youthful offenders who are placed in criminal court arrive there through some other method or legal procedure.

For example, even though complete national statistics are not available on youths who are statutorily excluded from juvenile court jurisdiction, police dispositions of juveniles that result in referral to adult court would appear to reflect the use of legislative waiver, as these offenders are treated as adults at the time of arrest. In 1996, near the height of nationwide concerns about youth violence and the implementation of many new legislative waiver laws, more than 81,500 juvenile offenders were referred to adult court by police, representing more than 6% of the total police dispositions for juvenile offenders during that year.[84] By 2001, the total had dropped to 51,000 offenders, which still represented 6.5% of the police dispositions for juveniles during that year.[85] Other evidence indicates that during the mid-1990s, about 200,000 youths were prosecuted as adults each year in the 13 states that set the upper age limit for juvenile court jurisdiction at 15 or 16 rather than 17.[86] These young offenders were tried in criminal court because they met the legal definition of adulthood in their respective states.

Current and complete national statistics also are not available on young offenders who end up in adult court as a result of prosecutorial waiver. In states that employ this method, however, juveniles transferred by a prosecutor are likely to outnumber judicially waived youths by a large margin. For example, Florida prosecutors transfer an average of nearly 5,000 offenders each year.[87] Other available data suggest that the number of annual prosecutorial waivers nationwide might be double or triple that of judicial waivers, and that prosecutorial waivers have increased more than fourfold since the late 1970s, far outpacing the growth in judicial waivers.[88]

In sum, the figures discussed above illustrate the modern trend, particularly during the mid-1990s, toward treating greater numbers of juvenile offenders as adults. Based on all available data, Donna Bishop estimated that in 1996 "at least 210,000 and as many as 260,000 offenders under eighteen were prosecuted in the nation's criminal courts.... This means that, nationally, 20–25 percent of offenders under age eighteen are treated as adults."[89] Although the total numbers seem to have dropped somewhat in more recent years, it would appear likely that roughly 200,000 youths under the age of 18 continue to be prosecuted in adult criminal courts under the various laws, methods, and procedures available today.

The basic rationale for the practice of sending hundreds of thousands of youthful offenders to adult court is that the juvenile court appears unable to serve the needs of certain young people, and, therefore, the criminal court should take over their cases. The perceived inability of the juvenile court to handle these cases may be based on a lack of faith in juvenile correctional facilities, a belief that harsher punishment is needed than can be provided in the juvenile system, or the view that some youths are too dangerous to remain outside the criminal system. Despite the recent shift in juvenile justice philosophy from the rehabilitative ideal to a more punitive orientation, the decision to transfer a case still denotes that a youthful offender is beyond whatever treatment capacity remains in the juvenile justice system.

Ironically, support for treating juvenile offenders as adults has come from both sides of the political spectrum.[90] "Due process liberals" assert that the informal and discretionary atmosphere that remains in many juvenile courts breeds discrimination and violation of constitutional rights. Consequently, they argue that rules of procedure in juvenile courts should be essentially the same as those in criminal court and more emphasis should be placed on the offense rather than the offender. Suggestions have continued to be made for doing away with the juvenile court altogether.[91] On the other hand, "crime control conservatives" believe that many of today's youthful offenders are no different than adult criminals and that the juvenile system provides neither effective rehabilitation nor adequate punishment required to ensure public safety. Therefore, they assert that these youths need to be prosecuted in the criminal system, where the goals of retribution, deterrence, and incapacitation can best be met.

To a certain extent, both groups have attacked the idea of a separate system of justice for juvenile offenders, but they use entirely different reasoning to support their position. A third group also can be added to the mix: supporters of the traditional juvenile court who would like to maintain a distinct system. These individuals see current reforms as an effort to "recriminalize delinquency," or return to the response to youthful offending that existed prior to the creation of juvenile courts.[92] Also, some do not accept criticisms of the rehabilitative ideal, arguing instead that past evaluations of treatment programs were weak and that many quality programs exist that produce positive results.[93] However, the overall nature of modern juvenile justice reforms shows that this third party has struggled to influence public policy.

JUVENILE TRANSFER IN PENNSYLVANIA

Legislative actions in Pennsylvania during the mid-1990s typified the way most states enacted laws at this time pertaining to a variety of juvenile justice issues, including the criminal prosecution of youthful offenders.[94] As with the rest of the nation, increasing youth violence in the state was receiving a great deal of public attention.[95] A newspaper editorial proclaimed:

> Violent crime among juveniles has reached alarming proportions in Pennsylvania. Teenage hoodlums, armed with deadly weapons, are terrorizing our streets and neighborhoods, committing senseless acts of brutality. Often their victims are other teenagers, but these young criminals ultimately prey on all of us, young and old alike.[96]

In response to this situation and amid much political fanfare legislators in Pennsylvania modified their juvenile code.[97] With the passage of Act 33 of 1995, a move was made away from the practice of judicial waiver and toward statutory exclusion. This was done with the expectation that the number of juveniles processed in adult criminal court would increase substantially. The way that Pennsylvania addressed the problem of youth violence, then, serves as an exemplar of the modern transfer movement.

Prior to March 1996, Pennsylvania's *Juvenile Act* provided that the transfer of juveniles to criminal court could occur through either judicial waiver or statutory exclusion.[98] However, the only crimes that fell under the legislative waiver component were those of murder and crimes committed by youths who were previously found guilty in a criminal proceeding for a misdemeanor or felony. Hence, for those juveniles who previously had never been found guilty in adult court, the act of murder constituted the only crime for which they could be statutorily excluded from juvenile court jurisdiction. Furthermore, the law also allowed for statutorily excluded youths to be returned to juvenile court for adjudication, disposition, or both (that is, reverse waiver), basically at the criminal court's discretion.

The more common method of transfer was judicial waiver, according to the standards set forth in *Kent v. United States* and in *Breed v. Jones*. Prior to transfer or any determination of guilt, a formal waiver hearing had to be held and a number of criteria had to be met. Objective criteria included a minimum age of 14 at the time of the alleged incident, the establishment of a *prima facie* case (that is, sufficient evidence) against the juvenile, and the classification of the alleged offense as a felony. If those criteria were satisfied, the juvenile court judge then had to determine that the youth was no longer amenable to treatment in the juvenile system. To do so, the judge was to consider the juvenile's age, mental capacity, maturity, degree of criminal sophistication, prior delinquency involvement, prior treatment experience, chances for rehabilitation, nature of the current offense, and any other relevant factors.

If the judge found that the youth was no longer amenable to treatment in the juvenile system, the case could be waived to adult court. In addition, the judge could transfer the proceedings at the request of the juvenile, as this request allowed the court to order the listed criteria as not applicable. In short, Pennsylvania's juvenile code granted judges the type of broad discretionary power to transfer cases that has been criticized in the past.[99] Under this system, from 1985 through 1995, approximately 1% of the total number of juvenile court dispositions in Pennsylvania resulted in a judicial waiver.[100] In terms of total judicial waivers during this time period, there was a gradual increase from 227 in 1985 (0.78% of the total dispositions) to 375 in 1990 (1.06% of the total dispositions) and finally to 533 in 1995 (1.44% of the total dispositions).

In 1995, in response to statewide (and nationwide) concern over increases in youth violence, significant legislative attention was given to the juvenile justice system in Pennsylvania. Subsequently, the Commonwealth's *Juvenile Act* was modified.[101] New legislation was enacted that pertained to such matters as the use of juvenile records in determining bail, fingerprinting of juveniles, expunging juvenile records, public access to delinquency hearings, restitution by youthful offenders, creation of a DNA database, background checks for gun purchases, parental participation in treatment programming, parental responsibility for truancy, and reporting of delinquency dispositions. However, probably the most important change concerned the prosecution of youthful offenders in adult criminal court.

Overall, the new *Juvenile Act* was structured to meet several objectives. This is evident in an opening statement of the code, which states that the purpose of the Act is:

> Consistent with the protection of the public interest, to provide for children committing delinquent acts programs of supervision, care and rehabilitation which provide balanced attention to the protection of the community, the imposition of accountability for offenses committed and the development of competencies to enable children to become responsible and productive members of the community.[102]

As part of this "balanced attention," the new juvenile code excluded from juvenile court jurisdiction any youth charged with murder or any of the following violent offenses when the child was between 15 and 18 years of age at the time of the alleged offense and a deadly weapon[103] was used during the offense: rape; involuntary deviate sexual intercourse; aggravated assault; robbery; robbery of a motor vehicle; aggravated indecent assault; kidnapping; voluntary manslaughter; or an attempt, conspiracy, or solicitation to commit murder or any of these other listed offenses. The new act also excluded any youth between 15 and 18 years old at the time of the alleged offense who commits any of the above-listed crimes, except for aggravated assault, after previously being adjudicated delinquent on the basis of any of these offenses.[104] Also, it is noteworthy that the revised juvenile code allowed for excluded cases to be transferred back to juvenile court if the offender establishes by a preponderance of the evidence that a reverse waiver will serve the public interest.

In addition to excluding the above designated violent felonies from juvenile court jurisdiction, the new act still permitted discretionary judicial waiver of cases.[105] Here, the burden of establishing by a preponderance of the evidence that the public interest is served by transferring the case to criminal court rests with the prosecution with two exceptions: if a deadly weapon was used and the youth was 14 at the time of the offense; or the youth was 15 or older, was previously adjudicated delinquent on the basis of a felony, and was alleged to have committed any of a series of designated felonies set forth in the juvenile act. If either of these last two criteria is met, the burden of establishing by a preponderance of the evidence that retaining the case in juvenile court would serve the public interest rests with the juvenile.

As with the former juvenile code, the revised act provides for two transfer mechanisms: judicial waiver and statutory exclusion. However, the focus is now clearly on the exclusion of violent offenders from juvenile court jurisdiction. Youths between 15 and 18 years old who commit a violent offense with a deadly weapon, as well as some repeat violent offenders, essentially receive "automatic adulthood." In addition, a presumptive waiver component was added to the traditional judicial waiver process, again with a focus on offenses committed with a deadly weapon and repeat offenders. Overall, the amended juvenile code in Pennsylvania corresponds well with the nationwide shift toward a more retributive model of juvenile justice, as it emphasizes holding youths accountable for violent offending.

SUMMARY AND CONCLUSIONS

Despite the juvenile court's traditional emphasis on treatment, rehabilitation, and serving the best interests of children, the practice of transferring certain young offenders to adult criminal court has been in existence since the creation of a separate system of juvenile justice. In fact, waiving more serious and violent offenders to adult court was part of the process of juvenile courts establishing their purpose and legal foundation. For roughly the first two thirds of the twentieth century, discretionary judicial waiver served as the primary method of transfer, often taking place in an informal environment lacking procedural due process protections. In the late 1960s and early 1970s, several U.S. Supreme Court rulings sought to change the way juvenile courts were operating, including the manner in which offenders were being sent to the adult criminal system.

At the same time that the due process revolution in juvenile justice occurred, crimes committed by young people were rapidly increasing, and the effectiveness of common rehabilitative programs was being seriously challenged. These factors all contributed to an increased emphasis on just deserts and getting tough with those who violate the law, and calls even were made for abolishing the juvenile court. Dramatic increases in youth violence from the mid-1980s through the mid-1990s fueled further efforts to crack down on juvenile crime, and virtually all states responded by passing new laws intended to facilitate the transfer of serious and violent offenders to adult court. Today, various prosecutorial and legislative waiver strategies exist along with revised judicial waiver practices and other transfer procedures, and somewhere in the neighborhood of 200,000 offenders under the age of 18 are processed in the adult criminal system each year in the United States.

Juvenile transfer to adult court is popular, then, in both policy and practice. Furthermore, during the past 30 years, a growing body of research has been produced in this area. In the following chapters, we will examine findings from empirical studies on transferred youths, covering the characteristics of waived offenders, case outcomes in adult court, deterrent effects, and the nature of contemporary punishment and rehabilitation efforts directed at serious and violent youthful offenders. Overall, much of this research has questioned the efficacy of this practice. A major goal, therefore, will be to clarify the available empirical findings and present examples and conclusions that can be considered by future policymakers and in public discussions of the topic.

CHAPTER 4

Who Gets Transferred?

With the traditional judicial waiver approach, judges have been granted a great deal of discretion in determining whether to send a case to adult court. Prosecutorial waiver shifts much of this discretion to a prosecuting attorney. Even with the currently used legislative waiver and mandatory judicial waiver proceedings, discretion exists at the charging stage and with such current strategies as reverse waiver and blended sentencing. The discretionary decision-making present across virtually all methods of transfer has caused many to question whether arbitrary or discriminatory decisions are characteristic of this practice.

During the past few decades, a substantial amount of research has focused on the demographic, legal, and social characteristics of waived youths. In general, these studies have sought to identify key offender traits in order to provide an understanding of the types of offenders affected by transfer provisions and to assess procedural fairness. Offense seriousness, prior record, age, and race have been considered most often; relatively fewer researchers have investigated the effect of such variables as geographic location, school status, and weapon use. Some studies have been done on a statewide or local basis, while other data exist at the national level. Finally, much of this research has been descriptive in nature (that is, simply reporting on the characteristics of waived juveniles), while more recent comparative and multivariate (that is, considering numerous explanatory variables and their potential impact on the likelihood of transfer) studies have sought to better distinguish transferred and non-transferred youths and to identify significant legal and extralegal factors in the transfer decision.

In determining which youthful offenders are most likely to get transferred to adult criminal court, it is useful to consider the discretion built into the various methods of waiver and how successful efforts have been to reduce or redirect this discretion. The case of Nathaniel Abraham further illustrates how demographic, legal, and social factors impact on the transfer process and how discretion continues to play a large role in this practice.

CHARACTERISTICS OF WAIVED YOUTHS

Most of what is known about the characteristics of transferred youths has been revealed in studies of judicial waiver that were based on data collected at the local, state, and national levels. Fewer studies have examined the traits of juveniles transferred through prosecutorial waiver, and very little research of this type has been done on legislatively waived offenders. Overall, though, this body of literature has been somewhat successful in identifying who gets transferred, what behaviors influence their transfers, and whether changes in the characteristics of waived youths have occurred in recent years.

Demographic Characteristics

In general, harsher juvenile court sanctions tend to be associated with older youthful offenders rather than younger ones who are processed earlier in their delinquent careers.[1] Because transfer to adult court commonly is viewed as both a severe juvenile court disposition itself and as a way to increase subsequent punishment severity, age would be expected to have a positive impact on the likelihood of waiver. Moreover, older juvenile offenders have less time remaining under juvenile court jurisdiction and being viewed as "almost an adult" might further increase a youth's chances of being sent to the adult criminal system. Research to date provides strong support for the relationship between age and transfer.

Descriptive studies using data from the 1970s and 1980s consistently suggested that older youths were more likely to be waived than younger offenders and that most waived youths were 17 years old.[2] Although informative, these studies failed to employ comparison groups of similar offenders retained in juvenile court and to simultaneously control for other factors beyond age that might impact on transfer to adult court. However, more recent comparative and multivariate research has confirmed the positive effect of age on the likelihood of transfer while taking into account a variety of other explanatory factors.[3]

It seems clear from studies to date that if all else is equal, older juvenile offenders are more likely to be transferred than are younger delinquents, and, in fact, those aged 16 and older continue to represent a solid majority of all waived youths.[4] Nevertheless, as noted by Donna Bishop, increasing use of legislative and prosecutorial waiver in recent times does appear to have increased the transfer of younger adolescents.[5] A central aspect of many modern waiver laws is the establishment of lower minimum ages for transfer, particularly in cases of mandatory or automatic waiver, which results in greater numbers of younger offenders being sent to the adult system. What is not well understood, however, is the extent to which age impacts on the decertification, or reverse waiver, of youths back to juvenile court. Limited research suggests that younger offenders are more likely to be decertified than are older youths initially sent to adult court,[6] but more investigation is needed into this aspect of juvenile transfer.

Along with age, race has been an often studied but more controversial demographic characteristic that potentially plays a role in the transfer process.[7] Virtually all studies that measure the race of waived offenders find that nonwhites (especially African Americans) are highly overrepresented, usually making up 50% to 95% of transferred youths.[8] These numbers hint at racial bias because only 15% to 20% of all juveniles are nonwhite yet nonwhite youths account for roughly 30% of all juvenile arrests, 45% of all juvenile arrests for violent index crimes, and 35% of all juvenile court referrals.[9] Relatively few studies, though, have examined the possibility of a race effect on the transfer decision while controlling for other potential explanatory factors.

Some early evidence did indicate that race appeared to exert a significant influence on the likelihood of waiver to adult court.[10] These studies, however, did a rather poor job of accounting for offense seriousness and prior record in considering differences in transfer based on race. However, more recent research with stronger controls for offense seriousness, prior record, and other factors has failed to uncover any direct race effect.[11] In other words, this research generally suggests that nonwhites are over-represented in overall transfer figures because of greater offense serious-ness, a more extensive prior record, or both.

Still, it seems that the effect of race could be more indirect than direct, as the decision to transfer generally comes later in the juvenile justice process and in a youth's delinquent career.[12] To illustrate, a juvenile's prior record may be affected by police response to juvenile crime, and police response may be influenced strongly by neighborhood social con-text and the status of minority group members.[13] This means that non-whites could have greater prior records as a result of differences in the way police enforce the law in various communities. Furthermore, other research focusing on juvenile arrest, intake, detention, adjudication, and disposition has found evidence of racial bias operating in these stages of processing.[14] In sum, as stated by M. A. Bortner and colleagues, "research has fairly consistently shown that small effects of race and class that might not be statistically significant at a given stage add up across multiple stages, with the effect that white and middle-class children are more likely to be filtered out of the system long before the transfer decision is reached than are poor youths and youths of color."[15]

A final demographic characteristic to consider is gender, as "virtually all respondents waived from juvenile to criminal court are male."[16] A variety of studies using local and statewide data support this conclusion.[17] National data also indicate that about 95% of all transferred youths are male.[18] Although offense seriousness and prior record likely explain much of this gender disparity in juvenile waiver, the low numbers of females available for study often lead to male-only samples and ana-lyses,[19] and the possibility of a gender effect on the likelihood of transfer does exist.

Overall, the typical juvenile offender transferred to adult court is an older, male, and nonwhite (often African American) adolescent. Al-though socioeconomic status is not a well measured or frequently studied characteristic in waiver research, few would argue with the statement that transferred youths are typically poor, inner-city offenders. However, al-though urban juveniles tend to make up a solid majority of all waived youths, it actually appears that rural youths may be more likely to be trans-ferred than comparable urban offenders.[20] Perhaps this is the result of a higher threshold in urban juvenile courts for defining serious offending or it may be that rural juvenile courts have less access to treatment programs and secure correctional facilities.

Legal Factors

As noted in the previous section, offense seriousness and prior record are two important factors to consider in assessing who is most likely to be transferred to adult court. With this in mind, a substantial amount of research has examined the offense characteristics of waived youths. Somewhat surprisingly, studies using data collected in the 1970s and 1980s generally indicated that the largest percentage of transferred offenders had been charged with property offenses but they tended to exhibit rather lengthy offending histories.[21] Even into the early 1990s, when violent crimes were becoming a central focus of juvenile justice attention, violent offenders continued to be outnumbered by property offenders in national waiver statistics.[22]

Studies conducted since the early 1990s, however, show that this situation has changed. Rising youth violence became a greater national concern, and new and expanded waiver laws were enacted that tended to focus on violent offenders. By the mid-1990s juveniles charged with personal or violent crimes comprised the largest percentage of waived youths.[23] Although this trend seems to have reversed itself recently in terms of judicial waivers so that property offenses again constitute a greater share of waived cases than person offenses,[24] youths sent to the adult system via prosecutorial or legislative waiver far outnumber judicially waived offenders and are more likely to be charged with violent offenses.[25]

In addition to the descriptive research reported above, a number of comparative and multivariate studies have investigated, while controlling for other factors, the relative impact of offense seriousness and prior record on the likelihood of waiver to adult court. Results from several studies have suggested that the more violent the offense, the greater the chances of transfer.[26] A few others, though, have found less supportive evidence of the influence of offense seriousness.[27] One limitation inherent in much of this research is an inability to adequately control for victim injury in assessing the impact of offense seriousness. In other words, the extent of a victim's injuries may be viewed as more important in the eyes of judges and prosecutors than are such factors as the specific offense type or grade or whether a firearm was employed during the commission of the offense.

Findings concerning the impact of prior record on the likelihood of transfer are somewhat similar to those regarding offense seriousness. A number of studies, which account for other explanatory factors, have indicated that a more extensive prior record or prior offending history is associated with an increased risk of waiver.[28] However, studies done by Jeffrey Fagan and colleagues that have controlled for age of onset have found that having a prior record was not a significant predictor of transfer.[29] This means that youths in contact with the juvenile system at an earlier age were more likely to be waived and that age of onset explained away the expected relationship between prior record and transfer.

Undoubtedly, offense seriousness and prior record play some role in explaining which young offenders are sent to the adult system and which ones remain in juvenile court. It is likely that the effects of these variables differ somewhat from jurisdiction to jurisdiction and also depend on how well other important factors are controlled (for instance, victim injury, age of onset, or length of time the offender has been involved with the juvenile system). Furthermore, it is also possible that offense seriousness and prior record have an interactive effect on the likelihood of transfer. Although not well studied, youths who commit the most serious offenses and who also have substantial prior records would appear to be at the highest risk of being waived to adult court. Even so, as argued by Robert Dawson, prior record may have "an effect that is secondary to seriousness of the offense. For the most serious offenses, waiver does not depend upon whether there is a prior record. For less serious offenses, prior record becomes important in making the waiver decision. For the least serious offenses, it is the motivating reason for the prosecutor seeking waiver and, presumably, for the judge granting it."[30]

Other Variables

In addition to the demographic and legal factors discussed above, a few other important variables have been uncovered that potentially impact on the likelihood of transfer. In their study of 727 serious juvenile offenders processed in Virginia from 1988 through 1990, Poulos and Orchowsky actually found 13 significant predictors of judicial waiver to adult criminal court.[31] In addition to the positive effects of age and various measures of offense seriousness and prior record, two factors that decreased the chances of transfer were the educational level and mental health history of the offender. More specifically, if a juvenile had at least a ninth grade education or had a history of any mental health treatment, he or she was less likely to be waived than other serious offenders. These findings suggest that juvenile court judges are less likely to waive youths with greater educational attainment or prior mental health problems, and they appear to illustrate how the court's view of a youth as amenable to treatment or salvageable remains a key component of the transfer decision.

In one of the other stronger studies of the determinants of waiver to adult court, Podkopacz and Feld also found evidence that seemed to point to the importance of amenability to treatment in influencing juvenile court judges' transfer decisions.[32] In their study of 330 transfer motions filed in Hennepin County, Minnesota, between 1986 and 1992, "one of the most powerful variables ... was the recommendation given by court services personnel. When the probation officer and psychologist agreed on a recommendation either to retain juvenile court jurisdiction or to refer the youth to adult court, there was a statistically significant probability that the court would follow that advice."[33] Furthermore, the recommendation of the probation officer and court psychologist had to be in the same direction (either for or against transfer) for the effect to be observed. When the court officials disagreed, neither had a significant impact on the likelihood of transfer. This shows that when two professionals familiar with an offender agreed that the youth would be better served in juvenile court, transfer was significantly less likely to occur. On the other hand, when both opinions were in support of waiver, transfer became a "near certainty."

Along with the effect of the recommendations of probation officers and court psychologists, Podkopacz and Feld found that older youths and those with greater prior records and offense seriousness were significantly more likely to be waived to adult court. While these findings would be expected based on the results of other studies, this research also found that having a particular judge preside over the transfer process significantly impacted on the likelihood of transfer. In other words, while controlling for the other factors in the model, this research showed that youths appearing before a specific judge compared with all other judges as a group were significantly more likely to be waived. The authors concluded that "this finding is consistent with our contention that judicial waiver is a highly individualized, discretionary sentencing decision in which the outcomes depend significantly upon who is the judge."[34]

The findings of Poulos and Orchowsky, as well as Podkopacz and Feld, show that factors other than offense seriousness, prior record, and age do impact on the chances of transfer to adult court. However, even in these more sophisticated multivariate studies, only about 40% of the variation in the likelihood of waiver was accounted for by the independent variables in the models.[35] Roughly 60% was left unexplained, meaning that other unmeasured factors actually accounted for a majority of the variation observed in the likelihood of transfer. These other important variables could include such things as demeanor of the offender, type of counsel (public defender versus private attorney), victim injury or victim preference, and police officer recommendation. None of these factors have received much attention in research assessing the determinants of waiver. Interestingly, as discussed in the next section, many modern waiver laws can be seen as an attempt to limit the consideration of anything beyond offense seriousness, prior record, and age in deciding which juvenile offenders should be sent to adult criminal court.

DISCRETION IN THE TRANSFER PROCESS

The conclusions of Podkopacz and Feld regarding the importance of having a particular judge illustrate the ongoing concern about discretionary decision-making, a key issue in transfer policies and procedures. To begin, proponents of judicial waiver argue that the juvenile court is most able to consider the individual factors associated with a particular youth and to make an informed decision on whether the offender is best served by remaining in juvenile court or if transfer to adult court is warranted.[36] This approach generally is thought to be consistent with the traditional juvenile court philosophy that emphasizes individualized treatment and serving the best interests of children and youths. However, critics contend that juvenile courts lack the necessary skills, tools, and abilities to effectively assess amenability to treatment and to predict dangerousness and that the discretion inherent in judicial waiver proceedings allows for abuses and inequities to occur.[37]

By the late 1980s and early 1990s, it became apparent to many that the U.S. Supreme Court decisions in *Kent v. United States* and in *Breed v. Jones* and the guidelines that resulted were insufficient in guiding judicial waiver decision-making. With the corresponding rise in youth violence, others suggested that the juvenile system could no longer provide effective treatment programs to the new generation of serious and violent youthful offenders[38] and that reduced juvenile court discretion was needed in the waiver process to ensure public safety. Consequently, as discussed in Chapter 3, mandatory and presumptive waiver components were added to many existing judicial waiver laws, the use of prosecutorial waiver increased, and legislative waiver became a very popular method of automatically sending certain specified youths to the adult criminal system. As summarized by transfer researcher Donna Bishop, legislative and prosecutorial waivers have overtaken judicial waiver as the primary transfer mechanisms employed, which perhaps will lead to judicial waiver becoming obsolete in the near future.[39] The appeal of these two procedures lies in their perceived ability to circumvent the juvenile court and provide greater uniformity and consistency to transfer processes, as well as their symbolic importance within the "get tough" political agenda.

Discretion Redirection

Essentially, the move toward legislative and, to a lesser extent, prosecutorial waiver was an effort to reduce the transfer decision to a brief consideration of age, offense seriousness, and prior record. Under many modern and broad waiver laws, youths of a specified minimum age (for example, 15) who commit certain crimes (often violent felonies) or possess more substantial prior records are treated as adults soon after arrest rather than being referred to juvenile court for a more individualized assessment. This approach was expected to provide a more uniform and effective transfer process that ensured "deserving" offenders were quickly placed in the adult system. Unfortunately, other problems associated with administering this system and with the shifts in discretion that occurred were not as apparent to policymakers.

Legislative waiver laws tend to be rigid and over inclusive, and prosecutorial waiver statutes provide enhanced transfer powers to typically crime-control-oriented attorneys, who may be inexperienced and minimally informed about juvenile cases. Because of this, both approaches usually require corrective mechanisms to allow some initially waived cases to be returned to juvenile court.[40] These corrective measures come in the form of the decertification procedure, also known as reverse waiver, which was discussed in Chapter 3. As the decision to send an offender back to juvenile court commonly is made in adult criminal court, many modern transfer laws have, in effect, moved discretion and judicial decision-making from juvenile court to adult court.[41] This shift in discretion received little attention prior to the implementation of contemporary waiver laws, and policymakers and the general public seemed to assume that decertification would be a little-used mechanism judiciously employed by well-informed adult court judges.

In reality, "criminal court judges are already overworked and lack special expertise in dealing with young offenders. Moreover, criminal court judges are frequently given little guidance in exercising their discretion to return cases to the juvenile court or to impose juvenile sanctions."[42] Consequently, what often transpires appears similar to traditional juvenile court and judicial waiver proceedings except that decisions are made in adult court by individuals (most notably judges) with limited knowledge about and experience with specific offenders and juveniles in general. Some cases are dismissed early in the criminal court process because of a lack of evidence or other reasons; others are decertified to juvenile court, presumably after a consideration of offense seriousness, prior record, and amenability to treatment in the juvenile system; and the remaining cases proceed to trial or result in guilty pleas followed by sentencing. Even at the sentencing stage, though, a few states allow for defendants to be returned to the juvenile system for correctional purposes.[43]

Research Findings

A general view has emerged that many adolescent offenders are sufficiently different from adult criminals in cognitive and psychological development that they should not be processed in the adult criminal justice system[44] and that adult court judges and other officials know too little about adolescent development and the treatment services available to youthful offenders to adequately process their cases.[45] Still, relatively little is known about the decertification of initially waived youths, be it prior to or following a determination of guilt in adult criminal court. In fact, to date only two studies have examined the reverse waiver process. One used data from the late 1970s through the mid-1980s, and the other is more recent but limited in terms of the information it provides.

Simon Singer analyzed the case outcomes of 9,937 serious and violent adolescent offenders arrested in the state of New York from September 1978 through May 1985. In 1978, a new legislative waiver law statutorily excluded these youths from juvenile court jurisdiction and automatically placed them in adult court.[46] Of the nearly 10,000 offenders examined, almost 45% had their charges dismissed, about 30% were decertified to juvenile court, and only 25% were convicted in criminal court. A multivariate analysis of the determinants of "removal to juvenile court" for 7,803 of the offenders revealed that younger juveniles and females were significantly more likely to be decertified, while those exhibiting greater offense severity and prior records were less likely to be sent back to juvenile court. Also, New York City counties returned 34% of their 6,722 processed juveniles through reverse waiver, compared with only 10% of the 1,081 offenders in non–New York City counties.

Similar findings were produced by Snyder, Sickmund, and Poe-Yamagata in their more recent study of violent youths excluded from juvenile court under a legislative waiver law implemented in Pennsylvania during March 1996.[47] Of the 473 offenders, almost 20% had their charges dismissed early in the adult court process, and 30% were decertified to juvenile court. About 25% of the cases were dismissed later, which means that only around 25% of the original cases resulted in an adult court conviction. These figures are strikingly similar to those produced by Singer in his earlier study in New York. Moreover, despite a lack of multivariate analysis, Snyder and colleagues reported descriptive findings suggesting that younger and white youths were more likely to be decertified, while those who used a gun (as opposed to some other weapon) and those with greater prior records were more likely to remain in adult court.

In general, the findings of this research are consistent with those of studies that have examined the characteristics of transferred youths and the key predictors of waiver to adult court. An older, male offender from an urban area who possesses greater offense seriousness and prior record constitutes the typical youth actually handled in adult court, regardless of the method of transfer. Also, this research suggests that a solid majority of cases processed through legislative waiver are either dismissed or decertified to juvenile court. These findings, when considered along with those of other studies reviewed in this chapter, should cause one to question whether much is gained by shifting discretion from traditional judicial waiver practices to the proceedings in adult court that are associated with legislative and prosecutorial waiver. As stated by Snyder and colleagues, the "numbers suggest that the ultimate impact of Pennsylvania's exclusion legislation in 1996 was to retain in criminal court those cases that the juvenile court would have judicially waived had it been given the opportunity."[48] The difference, however, is that individuals with less knowledge and experience with juvenile offenders are now making many of the key decisions in the transfer process.[49]

THE CASE OF NATHANIEL ABRAHAM

The characteristics and circumstances surrounding the case of Nathaniel Abraham provide a good illustration of much of the information presented in this chapter. As previously mentioned, Nathaniel was 11 years old when he shot and killed an older adolescent near a suburban Detroit convenience store.[50] Thereafter, as perhaps the youngest murder defendant to be tried as an adult in American history,[51] Nathaniel was prosecuted under a new and unique state law that enabled youths younger than 14 to be charged as adults for certain serious and violent crimes, but the proceedings actually took place in juvenile court. At age 13, he was convicted of second-degree murder. As discussed below, presiding Oakland County Juvenile Court Judge Eugene A. Moore had several options for sentencing in this case, and it appears likely that his ultimate decision was based on a consideration of a variety of factors.

Nathaniel, being only 11 years old at the time of the offense and tried as an adult, provides an example of how modern transfer laws have lowered the minimum age for this practice. Although older youths are more likely to be waived than younger offenders, expanded prosecutorial and legislative waiver laws do increase the number of younger defendants who are tried as adults.[52] Nathaniel also was an African American male who committed a very serious offense (with a deadly weapon), and, despite little prior juvenile court involvement, he exhibited an alarming history of delinquent and violent behavior. In fact, Oakland County Prosecutor David Gorcyca reported that "Nate had 22 police contacts, five involving a gun. He took a gun to two different students and pointed it at two other students.... He also chased a bus driver down with it. He also beat a 14 year old over the head with a steel pipe."[53]

Based on Nathaniel's gender, race, offense seriousness, and history of offending, he represents the typical youthful offender treated as an adult in this country. At face value, only his young age stands out as unusual, and for many people the seriousness of the offense and Nathaniel's extensive offending history would be more important to consider than the fact that he was not yet a teenager. Indeed, this is exactly what Michigan's newly enacted law encouraged, as "there was no minimum [age] set for the statute under which Nathaniel was charged."[54] However, it might be worthwhile to think about factors beyond offense seriousness and prior record, which, it appears, is what Judge Moore actually did.

Nathaniel was born in 1986 and raised by a single mother, along with an older brother and sister.[55] He began exhibiting a pattern of difficult behavior at a young age, apparently suffered from attention deficit disorder and emotional impairment, and he received only a few sessions of counseling in an effort to treat these problems.[56] One of his teachers reported that Nathaniel did not understand the difference between fantasy and reality, and "he was determined to be functioning between the 6 and 8 year old level in terms of emotional maturity, internalized norms for appropriate behavior, and the acceptance of responsibility for his behavior."[57] In addition to these individual characteristics, Nathaniel grew up in an economically distressed and drug-infested neighborhood,[58] despite living in one of the wealthiest counties in America.

With this information in mind, by law Judge Moore had three sentencing options to consider (that is, he possessed a great deal of discretionary power). First, he could have sentenced Nathaniel strictly as an adult. If this route would have been chosen, state sentencing guidelines recommended eight to 25 years in a state prison.[59] Second, he could have sentenced Nathaniel solely as a juvenile, which would require his release from a juvenile correctional facility by the age of 21. Third, a blended sentence could have been imposed, which would have enabled placement in a juvenile facility followed by a transfer to an adult correctional facility if Nathaniel was not rehabilitated after eight years.

After much deliberation, Judge Moore chose the second alternative of a juvenile sentence and committed Nathaniel to a boys training school until the age of 21. In doing so, he stated that Nathaniel must be "accountable and responsible for his behavior," but he also reflected on history and suggested a different approach to dealing with juvenile crime:

> If we don't want to throw out the baby with the bath water, treat all youngsters more harshly, and perhaps even abolish the juvenile court and return to the days of the Industrial Revolution where we had one criminal court for both children and adults, we must do better with the thousands of juveniles we see every day in our juvenile courts. This county must

be willing to pay in dollars and human energy to help prevent juvenile crime and rehabilitate our young offenders. The media, the defense bar, the prosecutor, the judges, court and institutional staff, county commissioners, volunteers and the people of our community can and must make a difference. Children are too precious to be lost because of the system's neglect and failures.[60]

In leading up to his decision, Judge Moore also stated that treatment is more extensive and comprehensive in the juvenile system and that this system has a much higher success rate than the adult system. He argued further that adult prison should only be used as a last resort, incarceration does nothing to address future criminality, and in the adult system Nathaniel might be subjected to brutalization that could destroy any hope for rehabilitation. In sum, the judge in this case made a very important and symbolic decision that was influenced not only by the characteristics of the offense and the offender but also by his views concerning differences between the juvenile and adult systems and the general effectiveness of treating juveniles as adults. We will examine more thoroughly the validity of his beliefs in upcoming chapters.

SUMMARY AND CONCLUSIONS

Research indicates that the typical youth transferred to adult court tends to be older, nonwhite, and male and often comes from a poor, urban community. Furthermore, greater offense seriousness and a more substantial record of prior offending are associated with a higher likelihood of transfer. Modern waiver laws, which commonly focus on offense seriousness and prior record, also have increased the number of younger offenders who are sent to adult court. However, age and other factors related to amenability to treatment (such as school status, mental health problems, and recommendations from probation officers and psychologists), which were given strong consideration under traditional judicial waiver provisions, may still be working to influence the decertification or reverse waiver of youths who initially were remanded to adult court under contemporary legislative and prosecutorial waiver strategies.

Although not highly anticipated or studied in depth through scientific research, it appears that the recent shift from judicial waiver to legislative and prosecutorial waiver mainly has resulted in discretion being moved from the juvenile court to the adult court, and, in fact, that a large percentage of initially transferred cases either are dismissed or decertified by criminal court judges. Although the end result may be that those cases that proceed to prosecution are, for the most part, the same ones that would have been judicially waived by juvenile court judges in the past, it would seem that juvenile judges would possess more knowledge about individual offenders as well as delinquency and adolescent development in general in comparison to most adult court judges who are now making many of the key decisions in the transfer and reverse waiver process.

Finally, the case of Nathaniel Abraham shows how judicial discretion remains a key component of modern transfer laws and how offense and offender characteristics continue to be important in determinations about whether the juvenile or adult system should handle a particular case. Moreover, the judge's sentencing opinion in this case illustrates that concerns about differences in case outcomes, treatment and rehabilitation services, and the future criminal behavior of transferred and nontransferred youths play a critical role in decisions about which court system is more appropriate for an individual offender.

CHAPTER 5

What Happens in Adult Court?

There has been vigorous debate during the past 40 years with regard to the juvenile court's philosophy, structure, and procedures. A variety of critical attacks have focused on such issues as due process violations, ineffective treatment and rehabilitation services, abuse of the juvenile court's power, lenient treatment of adolescent offenders, and a general lack of direction in dealing with juvenile crime.[1] These criticisms, combined with rapid increases in youth violence from the mid-1980s to the mid-1990s and heavy media attention given to juvenile offending, have contributed to an erosion of the traditional juvenile court's philosophy and authority. A central issue is the transfer of juveniles to adult court, which often is described as a move toward "criminalizing" delinquent behavior.[2]

According to Peter Greenwood, one often hears the comment that youthful offenders receive only a "slap on the wrist" in juvenile court, and, in turn, this lenient treatment greatly contributes to overall levels of juvenile crime.[3] Those who favor expanded use of juvenile transfer to adult court tend to argue that this practice sends a message that the less severe sanctions of the juvenile system are no longer an option and that, instead, harsh criminal court sentences will be imposed. Through this harsher treatment, it is expected that offender accountability and public safety will be enhanced, while adolescent motivations to commit future crime will be diminished.

During the past 15 years, many states have amended their juvenile codes to emphasize the elements of accountability, retribution, and public safety.[4] At the same time that juvenile justice was becoming "tougher," a number of authors questioned whether the adult criminal system actually provides "better" punishment when handling youthful offenders.[5] One major expectation of sending serious and violent delinquents to adult court is that they will receive more certain and severe sanctions than they otherwise would be given in juvenile court. Unfortunately, although case outcomes of juveniles in adult court have been a major concentration of waiver research, studies on this topic have been of uneven quality, and the results from different pieces of research sometimes appear contradictory.

The case processing outcomes of adolescents in adult criminal court, and the differences that may or may not exist between comparable youths processed in the juvenile and adult systems are important to consider. Initial case processing stages, assessments of the likelihood of conviction and incarceration, length of incarceration, and case processing time must all be considered. The evidence available on case outcomes is not only important in thinking about the differences between juvenile and adult courts, but it also provides a useful context for discussing the nature and effectiveness of punishment and treatment in the two separate systems as well as the deterrent effects of transferring juveniles to adult court, which will be discussed in the following chapters.

INITIAL CASE PROCESSING

In comparison to subsequent stages of case processing, relatively little research has been done that investigates the initial handling of juveniles waived to adult court. Considering that increased accountability, punishment, and public safety tend to be major goals of juvenile transfer, most would expect that waived youths typically would remain in secure custody while awaiting trial. It is ironic, then, that the few studies that have examined the initial case processing of waived offenders have found that many or most of these youths actually are released from custody prior to trial, during which time they may receive little or no supervision or treatment. Moreover, further research suggests that violent youthful offenders in the adult system are more likely to be released from secure custody prior to disposition of their cases than are similar offenders in the juvenile system and that those adolescents who do remain in custody in adult jails experience greater negative consequences compared to similar offenders in juvenile detention facilities.

Release Estimates

Available national data indicate that slightly more than half of all juvenile felony defendants in adult criminal courts are released prior to final disposition of their cases. More specifically, using 1990, 1992, and 1994 data from the United States' 75 largest counties, Strom, Smith, and Snyder found that 51% of the roughly 1,500 offenders examined were released prior to final disposition.[6] Nearly 75% of the property offenders were discharged, along with 44% of the violent offenders.[7] These figures were generally lower than those pertaining to more than 370,000 youths processed in the juvenile courts of the same 75 counties. Of these juveniles, 65% were released prior to final disposition, including 71% of the property offenders and 57% of the violent offenders. However, no multivariate analysis was conducted to control for differences between the juvenile and adult court adolescents (for example, differences in prior record, offense seriousness, and age).

In a more recent study of almost 7,000 juvenile felony defendants processed in the criminal courts of 40 of the United States' largest counties in 1998, Rainville and Smith reported that 52% were released prior to final disposition, including 60% of the property offenders and 46% of the violent offenders.[8] Furthermore, of the nearly 3,500 offenders who were discharged, about half were let go under a nonfinancial arrangement (personal recognizance, unsecured, or conditional release). Unfortunately, no comparison data of similar youths retained in juvenile court was provided in this study.

Comparative Research

In an effort to provide a more sophisticated analysis of the predictors of release from secure custody for serious and violent youthful offenders, I previously examined a sample of 557 violent males from Pennsylvania who were processed in 1994.[9] These adolescents all were charged with robbery or aggravated assault, and a deadly weapon was involved in every offense. Subsequently, 138 of the offenders were judicially waived to adult court and 419 were retained in juvenile court, but all of them would have been excluded from juvenile court jurisdiction under the Act 33 legislative waiver law that was implemented in 1996 (as discussed in Chapter 3).

My initial results showed that, somewhat similar to available national figures, 55% of the transferred violent offenders were released from secure custody prior to final disposition. However, only 35% of the violent youths in juvenile court were allowed a similar release, a statistically significant difference of 20 percentage points. In addition, a multivariate analysis that controlled for a variety of legal and extralegal factors also revealed that waived adolescents were more likely to be released than were comparable youths retained in juvenile court. Not only were transferred offenders more likely to be set free but so were those from urban counties (compared with rural and suburban counties). On the other hand, juveniles who used a firearm (compared with some other type of deadly weapon) were less likely to be released. In general, these findings suggest the presence of an initial "custody gap" for violent youths waived to adult court, but further research in this area is needed.

In the late 1990s, Donna Bishop and colleagues interviewed 95 serious and chronic adolescent male offenders in Florida, of whom 49 had been transferred to adult court and 46 were prosecuted in juvenile court.[10] Although there were many similarities in the ways that the youths experienced predispositional confinement in the juvenile and adult systems (for example, indifferent staff members or bleak and threatening environments), other reported differences existed. Many juveniles in detention centers told of significant attachments to at least one staff member, which was not the case in adult jails. Juvenile detention stays also were described as less stressful and shorter, while jail confinement was associated with greater separation from family and friends as well as a higher level of perceived danger. Finally, most transferred youths did not perceive themselves as hardened or dangerous criminals, but they believed that jail officials viewed them this way.

Overall, despite the fairly small amount of research that exists in this area, it appears that a majority of transferred youths are released from secure custody prior to final disposition of their cases and that similar offenders in juvenile court actually may be more likely to remain in custody while awaiting adjudication and disposition. These findings seem to conflict with the popular belief that juvenile waiver provides greater accountability, punishment, and public safety, at least in terms of initial case processing. Moreover, adolescents who do remain confined in adult jails awaiting trial appear to experience greater adverse circumstances than do comparable offenders housed in juvenile detention centers. It is also quite possible that experiences while in pretrial custody have an impact on the subsequent actions and behaviors of youths held in adult facilities.

Finally, it should be noted that the issue of "preventive detention" by juvenile as well as adult courts has been a controversial topic. In recent times, the use of detention prior to trial and sentencing has increased, but identifying the most appropriate youthful offenders to detain is no easy task. Research by Fagan and Guggenheim uncovered a high rate of false positives among New York youths who were identified as posing a serious predispositional risk but who did not reoffend, particularly when future offending measures were limited to violent crime.[11] Other evidence suggests that detained juveniles may later receive more severe dispositions than comparable nondetained offenders.[12] Therefore, although some research suggests an initial custody gap for juveniles transferred to adult court, other concerns surrounding the use of preventive detention also should be considered.

CONVICTIONS IN ADULT COURT

A number of researchers have examined conviction rates for juveniles transferred to adult court. Perhaps not surprisingly, most studies generally find high conviction rates among waived youths, typically in the range of 65% to 95%.[13] However, an important question is whether these conviction rates in criminal court are significantly different from those of similar offenders in juvenile court. Research addressing this issue is somewhat limited. Most studies on this topic have been descriptive and did not include any comparison group of youthful offenders retained in juvenile court or a multivariate analysis to control for differences between juvenile and adult court youths. Furthermore, as the following discussion reveals, better-designed studies have produced mixed results.

Comparative Research

Early research by Joel Peter Eigen focused on homicide and robbery offenders in Philadelphia.[14] Juveniles judicially waived to adult court in

1970 and 1973 were compared with youths retained in juvenile court, and transferred juveniles also were compared with a sample of adults originally charged in criminal court. Of the 75 youths waived on homicide charges, 89% were convicted in adult court, and 90% of those convicted were found guilty of first- or second-degree murder or voluntary manslaughter. Of the 79 youths retained in juvenile court, only 77% were adjudicated delinquent. Finally, 70% of the 200 adult homicide defendants were convicted in criminal court, and 89% of those convicted were found guilty of either first- or second-degree murder or voluntary homicide. Very similar results were obtained with regard to robbery offenders.

The evidence from Eigen's research would seem to indicate that violent youthful offenders are held to a higher degree of accountability in adult court than in juvenile court and that in criminal court they are even more likely to be convicted than similar adult defendants. However, there is good reason to doubt this conclusion because differences across the groups of offenders were not controlled for using multivariate analysis. For example, Eigen also found that youths who allegedly killed a white victim and those with a higher degree of participation in a homicide offense were more likely to be waived to adult court, which could explain their greater percentage of conviction. Also, the most serious and aggravated robberies were found in the transferred group. These factors were not accounted for in making the comparisons of conviction rates, meaning that the higher conviction rates for transferred youths could be a product of race of victim, offense seriousness, or other influences rather than court of jurisdiction.

Research conducted as part of the effort to evaluate the Violent Juvenile Offender Program of the federal Office of Juvenile Justice and Delinquency Prevention improved upon the early work of Eigen. In an initial report, Cary Rudman and colleagues examined 138 youths charged with violent offenses and considered for transfer in Boston, Newark, and Phoenix between 1981 and 1984.[15] Of the 138 juveniles, 71 were retained in juvenile court and 67 were waived to criminal court. An important finding was that the rate of criminal conviction was slightly greater for youths retained in juvenile court (95.5%) than for those transferred to adult court (92.2%). The key point here may be that all of the juveniles were actually considered for transfer, as the data suggested that "once a juvenile charged with a violent crime (with a prior violent or serious offense) is considered for transfer to adult court, he or she very likely will be convicted of a target crime irrespective of which court has jurisdiction."[16]

Later reports on the same program by Jeffrey Fagan and associates expanded the sample to include 201 violent youths considered for transfer in Boston, Phoenix, Newark, and Detroit during the same time period.[17] Of these juveniles, 125 were retained in juvenile court and 76 were transferred to adult court. Again, conviction rates were found to be similar in both court systems, although now a bit higher in criminal court (93%) than in juvenile court (86%). On the other hand, charge reduction was more common in criminal court, as the conviction rate for target offenses was slightly greater in juvenile court. Overall, "the results showed that sanctions are fairly certain for both waived and retained youths charged with violent felonies.... There is little doubt that youths are held accountable for violent crimes, irrespective of the judicial forum in which the case is adjudicated."[18]

More recent findings from my own research, however, are contradictory to these conclusions regarding the accountability of violent youthful offenders in juvenile and adult court. In my study of the 557 violent males processed in Pennsylvania in 1994, I found that 87% of the 138 transferred youths were convicted compared with only 62% of the offenders retained in juvenile court.[19] A subsequent multivariate analysis that controlled for other legal and extralegal factors confirmed that the waived adolescents were more likely to be convicted. Furthermore, of those youths who were convicted in either court, transferred offenders were significantly more likely to be convicted of the targeted offenses of robbery or aggravated assault (that is, the violent offense originally charged).

While the research discussed to this point has focused on violent youths, a few other studies have considered conviction rates for both violent and property offenders in the juvenile and adult systems. Research in St. Louis by Kristine Kinder and colleagues compared 111 males who were certified as adults on a variety of charges in 1993 with the same number of randomly selected males who were adjudicated delinquent for felonies in juvenile court.[20] A major limitation of this study was that 66% of the cases transferred to criminal court were not followed through to a determination of guilt. With this in mind, the authors reported that only 23% of the waived cases had resulted in conviction, while 74% of the cases retained in juvenile court resulted in an adjudication of delinquency. They also asserted that of the transferred cases still pending, many would most likely be dismissed.

Two other stronger studies also have considered both violent and property offenders. The first, by Fagan, examined 15- and 16-year-old robbery and burglary defendants from New York and New Jersey who were arrested during 1981 and 1982.[21] Four hundred youths from two counties in New York who were processed in criminal court were compared to 400 youths from two matched counties in New Jersey who were handled in juvenile court. Based on New York law,[22] the cases from the New York sample originated in adult criminal court, while New Jersey law allowed for the comparable cases to be processed in juvenile court.

Fagan found that for offenders from both jurisdictions, the rate of conviction was higher for burglary cases than for robbery cases. Furthermore, the burglary conviction rate in New Jersey's juvenile courts (66%) was insignificantly greater than the burglary conviction rate in New York's criminal courts (63%). In contrast, robbery cases in New Jersey's juvenile courts were significantly less likely (46% conviction rate) to result in conviction than were robbery cases in New York's criminal courts (56% conviction rate). Nonetheless, these mixed findings led Fagan to conclude, "Accountability for adolescent offenders in criminal courts was no greater than for those in the juvenile courts."[23]

Finally, research by Podkopacz and Feld examined 330 cases processed in Hennepin County, Minnesota, from 1986 to 1992.[24] In these cases, which involved both violent and property offenses, a prosecutor filed a reference motion for the juvenile court to consider transfer. This resulted in 215 cases being waived to criminal court, while the other 115 cases were retained in juvenile court. Although conviction rates were not emphasized in their study, the authors reported that 97% of the transferred cases resulted in conviction in criminal court, while only 86% of the retained cases resulted in an adjudication of delinquency. The authors went on to say, "Clearly, prosecutors experienced less difficulty establishing the guilt of those youths referred to criminal court. This suggests either that juvenile courts implicitly may screen waiver cases for their prosecutive merits, or that prosecutors may pursue less vigorously the juvenile cases in which they anticipate less penal pay-off for their efforts."[25]

The Likelihood of Conviction

As a whole, while recognizing differences in research designs, quality, and findings across the studies reviewed in this section, the available evidence suggests that the likelihood of conviction is fairly high and somewhat similar for serious and violent adolescent offenders in both juvenile and adult court. Although a few comparative studies (including my own) indicate that conviction rates are higher in criminal court, others show little difference[26] or even that conviction rates are greater in juvenile court. In any case, there is scant evidence that juvenile courts dismiss a high rate of the more serious cases that come before them. The differences that do exist in conviction rates between juvenile and adult courts also appear to pertain mostly to violent offenders, who seem more likely to be convicted in adult court.

Another important point, alluded to by Podkopacz and Feld, is that the studies discussed above were done at times and in jurisdictions where juvenile judges, prosecutors, and other court officials potentially were serving a screening function, meaning that the "most deserving" cases with the highest probability of conviction likely had a greater chance of being sent to adult court. This means that selection bias actually could explain away the differences in conviction rates that were uncovered between juvenile and adult courts, even in the rare studies where some other possible explanatory factors were controlled (for example, offense seriousness, prior record, or weapon use).

This possibility is further strengthened when one considers the findings of the two studies that have examined the decertification of legislatively waived youths. As discussed in the last chapter, both Singer and Snyder and colleagues found that of the offenders initially sent to adult court under new legislative waiver laws, roughly 45% were dismissed, 30% were decertified, and only 25% were convicted.[27] In other words, adult judges, prosecutors, and other court officials appeared to step into the screening role previously filled by the juvenile court.

INCARCERATION AND INCARCERATION LENGTH

A major expectation in the move toward facilitating the transfer of juveniles to adult court is that these youths will receive harsher punishment than they otherwise would have within the juvenile system. In general, this desire for more severe sanctions has been justified on the basis of greater retribution, incapacitation, and deterrence. A question of great importance, then, is whether transferred youths do receive more severe punishment than they would have experienced in juvenile court. Contrary to what one might expect, the evidence indicates that harsher sanctioning in adult criminal court is not guaranteed.

Research from the 1980s indicated the presence of a "leniency gap" for juveniles waived to adult criminal court because transferred offenders typically were not imprisoned and actually appeared to receive less severe sentencing than they would have in juvenile court.[28] Studies from this time period also suggested that youths in adult court were not viewed as serious offenders because of their younger age and inexperience compared with most adults appearing in criminal court. However, more recent research has begun to clarify this situation. One important issue is the difference between property and violent offenders; another is the measurement of sanction severity. Following the suggestions of Hagan and Bumiller,[29] various studies have examined both sentence type and sentence length for different types of defendants.

Sentence Type

Concerning the type of sentence imposed, various studies show that youthful property offenders tend to be treated leniently in criminal court, often receiving sentences of probation in lieu of incarceration.[30] On the other hand, juveniles convicted of violent offenses appear to be treated harshly in criminal court, where a jail or prison term commonly is imposed.[31] However, as with conviction rates, it is still somewhat unclear if these incarceration rates in criminal court are very different from those of similar offenders in juvenile court because only a few studies have employed juvenile and adult court comparison groups.

The previously discussed studies of Eigen, Rudman and colleagues, and Fagan and associates, which focused on violent youthful offenders, did find higher incarceration rates among juveniles transferred to criminal court. Specifically, Eigen reported that 87% of the juveniles convicted of murder in adult court were incarcerated compared with 76% of the convicted adults and 49% of the youths adjudicated delinquent in juvenile court.[32] Rudman and colleagues found that 90% of the waived juveniles who were convicted were also incarcerated, while only 77% of those who were adjudicated delinquent received a dispositional placement.[33] Finally,

Fagan reported that 89% of the juveniles convicted in criminal court were incarcerated compared with 84% of those adjudicated in juvenile court.[34]

These results are consistent with the findings from my research on the transfer of violent male offenders in Pennsylvania. Of the 378 youths convicted in either adult court (120) or juvenile court (258) in 1994, 96% were incarcerated in adult court compared to only 64% of those retained in juvenile court.[35] Again, a subsequent multivariate analysis controlling other legal and extralegal factors verified that the waived and convicted adolescents were substantially more likely to be incarcerated than their juvenile court counterparts. The only other significant predictor of incarceration was release from predispositional secure custody, as those who were released were less likely to later receive a sentence of incarceration.

A few other studies have compared sentence type for both violent and property offenders in juvenile and adult court. For example, Barnes and Franz examined data on all 206 youths considered for transfer between 1978 and 1983 in a northern California metropolitan area.[36] Almost half (47%) of the juveniles were transferred, and the rest remained in juvenile court. Further analysis revealed that the effect of waiver varied with type of offense. Violent offenders were more likely to be incarcerated in adult court than were comparable offenders in juvenile court, while property offenders were less likely to be incarcerated in criminal court than were similar youths in juvenile court.

More recent research, though, has failed to find the same effect for the type of offense. In Fagan's study of New York and New Jersey offenders, it was revealed that 46% of the youths convicted of robbery in New York criminal courts were sent to prison, while only 18% of the offenders adjudicated delinquent on robbery charges in New Jersey juvenile courts were incarcerated.[37] The findings for burglary defendants were nearly identical, as 46% of the youths convicted in criminal court and 24% of those adjudicated delinquent in juvenile court were incarcerated.

Similar findings were reported by Podkopacz and Feld, although the percentage of youths incarcerated was much higher in both the juvenile and adult criminal courts that were studied.[38] In their study, adult criminal courts incarcerated 93% of the youths convicted of a violent offense, while the juvenile court imposed confinement on 65% of the retained youths who were adjudicated for a similar offense. The adult courts also incarcerated 78% of the offenders convicted of property offenses compared to only 61% in juvenile court. Therefore, for both violent and property offenses, "criminal courts incarcerated youths convicted as adults significantly more often than did the juvenile court."[39]

Another recent study that considered sentence type for youths in juvenile and adult court was conducted by Bishop and colleagues.[40] These researchers compared 2,738 waived offenders in Florida who were transferred to criminal court on a variety of charges in 1987 with the same number of individually matched delinquents who were retained in the juvenile system. Although sentence type was not a major focus of the study (recidivism was the main outcome variable examined), the authors did report that transferred juveniles were more likely to be incarcerated than youths who remained in the juvenile system.

In sum, research that has examined the type of sentence imposed on juveniles treated as adults has produced evolving results. Earlier studies found evidence that juvenile offenders were receiving more lenient treatment in criminal courts, often including sentences of probation. More recent research indicates a change in this pattern, particularly for violent offenders. It seems that the increasing concern about youth violence in recent times not only resulted in a larger percentage of violent juveniles being transferred to adult court but also in a larger percentage of those transferred being incarcerated. However, the lingering problem of selection bias again needs to be noted. Many of the above studies employed weak or nonexistant controls for offense seriousness and prior record, meaning that the transferred youths may have been more likely to be incarcerated simply because they were more serious offenders. Still, as stated by Podkopacz and Feld, "Although the waiver process selects youths on the basis of seriousness, the differences in rates of dismissal, conviction, and incarceration between the two systems are striking."[41]

Sentence Length

Research on the second dimension of sanction severity, length of incarceration, has produced similar results. Various studies have shown that for those transferred youths who are incarcerated, lengthy sentences are common.[42] These studies found average jail and prison sentences ranging from one to five years or more, with the longest sentences imposed on violent offenders. However, the next question would be whether the periods of incarceration issued in criminal court are longer than those prescribed for similar offenders in juvenile court.

Several studies have, in fact, found evidence that lengthier sentences are imposed in adult criminal court. Eigen's research revealed that juveniles convicted in adult court on either homicide or robbery charges received longer periods of incarceration than did convicted adult defendants and youths adjudicated in juvenile court.[43] In the study by Rudman and colleagues, youths incarcerated by criminal courts received sentences five times longer than those imposed on offenders retained in the juvenile system.[44] Similarly, Fagan's analysis revealed that sentences of incarceration for juveniles in criminal court were four times longer than for youths adjudicated in juvenile court,[45] and Bishop and associates found a mean sentence length of 245 days for waived juveniles who were incarcerated compared with only 90 days for youths retained and placed by the juvenile court.[46]

In my research on the transfer of violent youthful offenders in Pennsylvania, for the 280 adolescents who were incarcerated in either adult (115) or juvenile (165) correctional facilities, the average minimum sentence length imposed in adult court was approximately 27 months compared with nearly 12 months in juvenile court.[47] A corresponding multivariate analysis, controlling for other legal and extralegal factors, also revealed significantly longer periods of incarceration being imposed in adult court. In this model, the only other significant predictor of incarceration length was firearm use, as those who used a gun during the commission of their offense received a longer sentence than those who used some other type of deadly weapon.

Jurisdictional age limits of juvenile courts vary among states, but the maximum age for supervision and confinement is most commonly set between 18 and 21.[48] The results discussed above suggest that youths incarcerated by adult courts experience substantially longer sentences than those imposed by juvenile courts because criminal courts are not limited by the jurisdictional age restrictions present in the juvenile system. However, this conclusion must again be tempered by the recognition of possible selection bias as well as the inconsistent findings of several other studies.

For example, Podkopacz and Feld reported that youths convicted as adults on violent offenses experienced longer sentences of incarceration than those imposed on juveniles who were adjudicated delinquent on similar charges, but those convicted in adult court on property offenses received shorter sentences of incarceration than comparable offenders in the juvenile system.[49] Even more interesting, Fagan's study of robbery and burglary offenders found no difference in sentence lengths for youths charged with either offense and incarcerated by either the criminal or juvenile court.[50] Irrespective of type of offense and court of jurisdiction, average minimum sentences of incarceration were approximately 11 months, and average maximum sentences were 31 to 34 months.

It also should be noted that the amount of time an offender actually serves in confinement may be considerably different than the length of sentence imposed by a criminal court. A study focusing on this issue by Fritsch and colleagues examined the imprisonment of waived youths in Texas.[51] The researchers examined 946 offenders transferred to adult court from 1981 to 1993 who then were sentenced to prison. The key finding was that these juveniles consistently received longer sentences than were available in juvenile court, but they served an average of only 27% of their original sentence (for example, an offender receiving a two-year sentence would only be incarcerated for about six months). When actual time served was taken into account, the waived youths rarely served longer sentences than were available in juvenile court.

Overall, it appears that transferred juveniles who are incarcerated do receive fairly lengthy sentences, particularly those waived on violent charges. Furthermore, these offenders commonly receive longer sentences of incarceration than those issued to comparable youths in juvenile court. However, as indicated by Fagan's research, this difference in sentence length is not always present. Furthermore, even when longer sentences are imposed, youths in the adult system may actually be incarcerated for the same or even shorter terms than their counterparts in the juvenile system.

CASE PROCESSING TIME

Compared with the conviction and sentencing of juveniles transferred to adult court, the length of time it takes for their cases to be processed has been much less studied. Within the juvenile system, though, questions have been raised regarding the speed at which cases are processed.[52] While the Sixth Amendment to the Constitution guarantees a "speedy and public trial" for anyone charged with a criminal offense, the definition of "speedy" is open to debate. Furthermore, despite the due process revolution in juvenile justice that extended various procedural rights to youthful offenders, the U.S. Supreme Court has not addressed the issue of speedy trial rights for juveniles in any substantive way. In general, case processing time is becoming an emerging point of emphasis in juvenile justice, as immediate interventions are being stressed as a response to delinquent behavior.[53] Therefore, it would seem important to know how rapidly comparable cases are processed in the juvenile and adult systems.

Research by Jeffrey Butts focused on the handling of delinquency cases during 1991 and 1992 by juvenile courts in 16 states.[54] The median time from referral to disposition was 40 days, while 26% of all cases had disposition times exceeding 90 days. However, formally petitioned cases had substantially longer disposition times than cases handled informally, as almost 40% of all petitioned cases required more than 90 days to reach disposition. In larger jurisdictions, nearly half of all petitioned cases had disposition times in excess of 90 days, and 22% required more than 120 days. Finally, nearly 40% of all cases that resulted in out-of-home placement or formal probation supervision required more than 90 days to reach disposition. The 90-day time period is important because it is the maximum disposition time recommended by various national standards.

This research suggests that the most serious cases take the longest time to process in juvenile court, often requiring three to four months or more to reach disposition. The next question would concern the case processing time of comparable offenders in the juvenile and adult systems. Although disposition times for serious offenders in juvenile court may not meet national standards, juveniles waived to adult court may be subjected to even longer periods of case processing. A review of the literature finds that only a few studies have addressed this issue.

John Lemmon and colleagues examined all youths judicially waived to criminal court in Pennsylvania in 1986.[55] For these 221 cases, the mean time from transfer to sentencing for convicted offenders was 8.5 months, while the median time was 7 months. Although no comparison group was employed, this evidence indicates case processing times well in excess of those discussed by Butts with regard to serious offenders in the juvenile system.

Several comparison studies also have revealed findings of more rapid case processing in juvenile court. In their examination of youthful offenders from St. Louis, Kinder and associates reported that at the time their research ended, all of the cases that had been retained in juvenile court had completed disposition, while 66% of the transferred cases were still pending.[56] In a stronger study of case processing in three states, Rudman and colleagues found that it took 2.5 times as long (246 versus 98 days) for a violent youth to be transferred, convicted, and sentenced than for a similar youth to be retained, adjudicated, and disposed in juvenile court.[57] Fagan's research across two states also reported more rapid action in juvenile court, as cases took 100 days on average to be disposed in New Jersey juvenile courts and 145 days to reach sentencing in New York's criminal courts.[58]

Finally, my research on violent youths processed in juvenile and adult courts in Pennsylvania during 1994 revealed significantly faster case processing in juvenile court as well.[59] While accounting for other legal and extralegal factors, the estimated processing time in adult court was 202 days compared to 47 days in juvenile court. Two other significant predictors of case processing time included release from predispositional secure custody and age at first referral. Not surprisingly, those offenders who were released from custody experienced lengthier periods of processing, as did those with an older age of first referral to juvenile court. A possible explanation for the latter finding is that youths with an older age at first referral may be seen as less serious offenders with shorter offending histories, causing their cases to be "put on the backburner" or otherwise delayed while plea bargaining is worked out.

In sum, while the case processing times of serious offenses in juvenile court have been questioned and criticized, it appears likely that comparable cases in adult criminal court take even longer to reach completion. Although relatively few studies have been done in this area, the findings are consistently in support of speedier processing in juvenile court. If there is benefit to be gained from a more rapid response to offending, then transferring greater numbers and types of adolescent offenders to adult court would seem counterproductive.

SUMMARY AND CONCLUSIONS

Proponents of transferring juveniles to adult court commonly emphasize the perceived advantages of greater accountability and stronger punishment. Research that has assessed how well these goals have been met has produced some surprising and mixed results, while some other findings have been as expected. Many studies have provided only descriptive statistics on case outcomes of waived youths, while a smaller amount of comparative and multivariate research has supplied more thorough evidence concerning the case outcomes of cohorts of youths in juvenile and adult court.

In the predispositional stage of processing, it seems ironic that the juvenile system actually may be harsher than the adult system with respect to the custody of serious and violent youthful offenders. Research to date indicates that a majority of transferred offenders are released from custody prior to final disposition of their cases and that violent youths in adult court are more likely to be released than are similar adolescents in juvenile court. Many waived youths are likely to be set free with little or no supervision by their family or the court, and they are also likely to experience lengthy periods of case processing time, potentially increasing the opportunity and risk of new offending. Those who do remain in custody in adult jails appear more likely to experience a variety of adverse consequences, which also may impact on the future criminal behavior of these detained youths.

Studies that have focused on the likelihood of conviction for transferred offenders have found fairly high conviction rates in adult court. However, better-designed studies employing comparison groups of similar offenders in juvenile and adult court have produced mixed results, with relatively little difference often found in the likelihood of conviction across the two court systems. Although there is some evidence that violent offenders are more likely to be convicted in adult court than in juvenile court, it is quite possible that this finding is explained by the fact that the juvenile court served as a solid screening arena and only sent the cases with the greatest likelihood of conviction to adult court. In any event, there is little evidence that juvenile courts do a poor job holding offenders accountable in the first several stages of case processing.

Early research on the sentencing severity of transferred youths unexpectedly revealed a leniency gap in adult court, with probationary sentences commonly imposed on many youths who did not seem to be viewed as serious offenders. More recent research indicates a change in this pattern, at least for violent offenders, who, when convicted, typically receive sentences of incarceration that are longer than those imposed on similar youths in juvenile court. Even these findings must be tempered, however, with the recognition that the juvenile court likely served the screening function that placed the offenders deemed most deserving in adult court, and that actual time served in the adult system may be very different than the sentence imposed in some jurisdictions.

Finally, it seems fairly clear that while case processing time is a concern in the juvenile system, adolescents in adult court typically experience substantially longer periods of case processing than do comparable offenders in juvenile court. During this time, they are likely to be either released back into the community with little or no supervision or remain detained in adult jails in an adverse environment, perhaps with little opportunity for treatment of drug and alcohol, mental health, or other problems.

In general, those who argue in favor of "adult crime, adult time" generally fail to recognize the limits of this approach and the complex nature of the distinctions between juvenile and adult court. Although there certainly are transferred youths who experience secure predispositional custody and lengthy prison sentences, many do not, and the evidence further suggests that the juvenile court does a better than perceived job holding offenders accountable and sending the highest risk or most deserving cases to adult court. Furthermore, many transferred youths who do experience adult time serve their sentences and are paroled back into the community while they are still in their late teens or early twenties, the well-known peak years of serious and violent offending. Therefore, the effectiveness of the punishment and treatment received by serious and violent adolescent offenders and the impact of juvenile transfer on overall juvenile crime and individual criminal behavior should be of central importance.

CHAPTER 6

Prospects for Punishment and Rehabilitation

Prior to the 1970s, rehabilitation was the central correctional goal of both the adult and juvenile justice systems.[1] Particularly in the 1950s and 1960s, considerable enthusiasm was voiced for treatment programs directed at rehabilitating juvenile delinquents and adult criminals.[2] During the 1970s, however, a number of factors contributed to a lack of faith and support for correctional treatment, and the dominant goals became retribution, deterrence, and incapacitation.[3] This shift was seen first in the criminal justice system, but by the 1980s similar views and practices were apparent in the juvenile system as well. Since then, the response in America to lawbreaking behavior has focused greatly on providing harsher punishment and getting tough with juvenile and adult offenders.

Proponents of transferring juveniles to adult court often assert that criminal processing is needed to ensure that adequate punishment is imposed. Although research findings are not always as expected with regard to the case processing outcomes of adolescents in adult versus juvenile systems, more serious and violent convicted offenders in adult court do tend to receive periods of incarceration that are sometimes lengthy. Moreover, for those offenders who stay in juvenile court, a more punitive philosophy exists than was in place throughout most of the twentieth century.[4] A central question, then, pertains to the effectiveness of this punishment-oriented approach to crime and whether the correctional sanctions and services provided to youths in the adult criminal system are more effective than those given to similar offenders in the juvenile system.

Reviewing trends and research on punishment and rehabilitation during the past 40 years, first within the criminal justice system and then in the juvenile justice system, reveals some interesting findings. The evidence of treatment effectiveness for serious and violent youthful offenders, with an eye toward determining which system supplies the best chance for positive behavioral change, must also be considered here. Finally, the State Correctional Institute at Pine Grove, a state prison in Pennsylvania designed to house violent youths sentenced by adult courts, offers an example of modern efforts to incarcerate and treat serious and violent adolescent offenders in the adult system.

THE GET TOUGH MOVEMENT IN CRIMINAL JUSTICE

Crime and punishment have been high on the list of public concerns and political agendas since the late 1960s, resulting in a variety of criminal justice reforms and transformations. In 1965, Lyndon Johnson established the President's Commission on Law Enforcement and Administration of Justice to study crime in the United States and the effect of the nation's response to it by means of the criminal justice system. As historian John Conley explains, "President Johnson had many reasons for establishing the Crime Commission, including rising crime rates and the fear of crime, increasing social disorders and riots related to the Vietnam War protests and Civil Rights movements, and the increasing pressure from the conservative wing of the Republican party to address the crime issue."[5] This commission subsequently produced a number of reports and eventually published *The Challenge of Crime in a Free Society* in 1967.[6]

While the President's Commission examined and wrote on a number of topics and operations (including policing, corrections, courts, juvenile justice, and others), it specifically noted a need to know more about crime and the effectiveness of justice system responses.[7] Although recommendations for an expanded research agenda could have been strengthened, the work of the commission marked a turning point in the growth and development of criminology and the use of scientific research to study crime and criminal justice.[8] The use of victimization surveys and police observational studies, for example, can be traced to the work of the commission. On the other hand, some of the commission's recommendations generally were ignored (for example, those in the area of corrections, where greater use of social reintegration was recommended),[9] while others had a relatively short-term impact (for example, those in the area of juvenile justice, to be discussed shortly).[10]

Crime and Justice in the 1970s

For a variety of reasons, America's growing interest in crime and justice accelerated in the 1970s. To begin, as the baby-boom generation entered their peak years of offending (that is, middle to late adolescence), increases in official crime that began in the mid-1960s continued well into the 1970s.[11] The country's crime problem soon became a major political issue, and crime control became a key aspect of partisan politics.[12] More specifically, political conservatives adopted the philosophy of getting tough on crime and blamed rising crime rates on lenient judges and soft sentencing standards. A liberal-to-conservative shift ensued with regard to responding to crime, and calls for more punitive punishments and lengthier prison sentences became a popular political practice.

Additionally, until the 1970s, indeterminate sentencing was the usual approach taken to impose sanctions on both adult and juvenile offenders. Within this system, prosecutors, judges, corrections officials, and parole boards had broad discretionary powers to process defendants and determine the nature and length of sentences imposed, in accordance with minimum and maximum times set by law.[13] In general, this was thought to encourage and allow for rehabilitation to take place, with various criminal justice system officials and practitioners attempting to ensure that it did. By the mid-1970s, though, civil-rights activists concerned with racial and class bias and sentencing disparities demanded controls on the discretion of judges and other officials.[14] This soon led to a shift toward determinate sentencing practices for the purposes of reducing discretion and supplying a known punishment length at the time of sentencing. Proceduralists in the legal system generally supported this change as a way to make legal processes fairer and decision makers more accountable. They further argued that sentencing should be subject to stricter rules and review procedures. Moves toward both mandatory sentencing, which seeks to require at least a minimum set punishment in response to certain specified crimes, and determinate sentencing were supported wholeheartedly by crime control conservatives in the get tough camp.

Finally, and perhaps most importantly, in the mid-1970s a large-scale review of correctional rehabilitation programs and their impact on future criminal behavior concluded that there was little scientific evidence that these programs successfully reduced future criminal behavior (that is, recidivism).[15] The conclusion that "nothing works" to rehabilitate criminals was used to support the move from indeterminate to determinate sentencing, and it also provided further evidence for those who believed that more punitive sanctions and a punishment-oriented system were needed. By the time a subsequent review of rehabilitation programs and their effectiveness that came to similar conclusions was published in 1979,[16] the goal of rehabilitation in criminal justice had been replaced by those of retribution, incapacitation, and deterrence.

Crime and Justice in Recent Times

During the past 30 years, official crime rates have fluctuated, but both violent and property crime rates are higher now than in the early 1970s.[17] During the same time, as a result of the shift toward a more punitive justice system, the use of incarceration increased dramatically. From 1972 until 2003, the overall incarceration rate grew from 93 per 100,000 residents to 715 per 100,000, and more than 2 million people are imprisoned in the United States today.[18] At the same time that jail and prison populations were rising, intermediate and alternative sanctions became popular as a way to try to provide adequate punishment while offsetting the surging costs of incarceration and burgeoning prison populations.[19] The most popular of these approaches tended to be those viewed as the "toughest," including boot camps, intensive supervision, and electronic monitoring.

It is important to note that the scientific evidence concerning the effectiveness of contemporary punishment-oriented strategies provides, at best, limited support for these methods.[20] For example, there is no doubt that incarcerating large numbers and many types of offenders prevents them from committing crime and leads to some overall crime reduction. Studies suggest, however, that this approach in the United States during the past 20 to 30 years has reduced crime by only about 10% to 20% while costing billions of dollars.[21] Furthermore, research on the popular and more punitive intermediate punishments employed generally finds no beneficial impact on future criminal behavior, and harsher forms of these sanctions (for example, disciplinary-style boot camps) even have been found to increase recidivism rather than reduce it.

At the same time that incarceration and other punitive sanctions came to dominate sentencing and corrections, rehabilitation and treatment services struggled to remain a component of criminal justice system operations. During the 1990s, though, there were signs of renewed interest in correctional rehabilitation among politicians, practitioners, and the general public.[22] The rising monetary cost of large-scale incarceration could no longer be ignored, intermediate and alternative sanctions did not appear to provide the anticipated beneficial effects on offender behavior and prison populations, and increasing concern was being generated about minority overrepresentation in correctional facilities. Furthermore, contemporary studies were suggesting that treatment and rehabilitation programs actually could be effective in reducing recidivism.[23]

Rediscovering Rehabilitation

More recent and optimistic assessments of the effectiveness of rehabilitation programs have been the result of several changes.[24] First, earlier conclusions about the ineffectiveness of various treatment interventions often were based on poorly designed research; more scientifically rigorous program evaluations in the 1980s and 1990s tended to produce more supportive results. Second, many programs that were studied in the past were poorly implemented and delivered in such a weakened format that little impact reasonably could be expected. Sound program implementation and maintenance of program integrity have emerged as important factors that typically are correlated with program effectiveness.[25] Third, modern research has established that the key issue is not whether something works but what works best for whom.

Studies have shown that treatment and rehabilitation programs should target higher risk offenders who potentially can benefit the most from the intervention, as the effects of treatment typically are greater among higher risk cases than among lower risk cases.[26] Furthermore, the services provided should focus on characteristics that can be changed (dynamic factors) and that have been associated with greater criminal behavior, such as antisocial attitudes, deviant peer associations, poor family interactions, and inadequate life skills. Finally, the style and mode of treatment delivered should match the learning styles and abilities of the participating offenders. In general, more effective rehabilitation programs tend to follow a cognitive-behavioral or social-learning approach rather than employing confrontational tactics or unstructured group or individual counseling.

As evaluation research, program implementation, and understanding of offender risk and needs have improved, a variety of rehabilitation programs have been identified that are effective in reducing criminal behavior.[27] Despite these supportive findings, punitive and incarceration-based sentencing strategies remain at the center of criminal justice system operations, and being tough on crime still dominates political platforms. Recent world events are focusing American attention on terrorism and homeland security, and a general strategy is emerging that emphasizes powerful defense, assertion of authority, and holding enemies accountable. Therefore, it would appear likely that a punishment-oriented criminal justice system will continue into the foreseeable future. In terms of juvenile justice, though, it is possible that a different approach will be taken.

REINVENTING JUVENILE JUSTICE

In earlier chapters of this book, the evolution of juvenile justice, juvenile courts, and transferring juveniles to adult court was examined. We will now focus on how the nature of punishment and rehabilitation for young people has changed during the past 40 years and how effective these efforts have been in correcting the behavior of serious and violent adolescent offenders. Further consideration will be made of the punishment and treatment received by juveniles who are tried and sentenced as adults.

The Four "D's" of Juvenile Justice

Juvenile justice and delinquency was a focal point of the President's Commission on Law Enforcement and Administration of Justice in the mid-1960s.[28] Increases in overall crime were being fueled by the behavior of teenage baby-boomers, and social unrest resulting from the Vietnam

War and conditions in urban areas further contributed to the view that a generation of young people was out of control. Furthermore, the fundamental principles of the juvenile court were being challenged on constitutional grounds and based on concerns about the conditions and practices of juvenile institutions. Rather than recommending a crackdown or a punitive approach to youth crime, the commission proposed that the juvenile justice system should be reformed in a way that minimized the labeling and stigmatization of offenders and also used more community-based prevention and intervention strategies.

Specifically, the President's Commission asserted that juvenile justice should embrace four "D's" for change: deinstitutionalization, diversion, decriminalization, and due process. Community corrections were viewed as a more effective alternative than custodial institutions, which had been criticized for poor living conditions and inadequate services. For most offenders, complete diversion from the juvenile court into community-based programs was recommended. In addition, status offenses were to be decriminalized and the jurisdiction of the juvenile court narrowed to reduce court involvement and the subsequent abuses of state guardianship. Finally, following up on the U.S. Supreme Court decisions in *Kent* and *Gault*, the commission supported expanded due process rights for juveniles.

Seven years after the publication of *The Challenge of Crime in a Free Society*,[29] the Juvenile Justice and Delinquency Prevention Act of 1974 was passed by Congress. This legislation incorporated many of the recommendations of the President's Commission. At this time, deinstitutionalization, diversion, decriminalization, and due process were thought to represent a revolution in juvenile justice. As stated by Alexander Pisciotta, "By the mid 1970s, many politicians, practitioners, academics, and child welfare advocates were confident that they had finally discovered the elixir for delinquency and youthful behavior—benevolent reform was, at long last, at hand."[30] To the surprise of many, then, this revolution was short-lived.

Juvenile Justice and the Rise of Get Tough

As previously discussed, in the mid-1970s, increasing crime rates, a shift to a conservative ideology, and reviews of research that strongly questioned the effectiveness of rehabilitation programs resulted in the rise of the get tough movement in criminal justice. The recommendations of the President's Commission and the resulting Juvenile Act of 1974 quickly came under attack,[31] and by the late 1970s, optimism about reforms instituted just a few years earlier was replaced by calls for increases in waivers to adult court, longer sentences from juvenile court, and the use of the death penalty for juveniles. By the early to mid-1980s, efforts to provide more punitive sanctions for juvenile delinquents became as popular as doing the same for adults, and calls were even made to do away with the juvenile court entirely.[32]

Similar to previous changes in the adult criminal system, in the 1980s juvenile codes across the county were revised for the purpose of enhancing public protection through determinate and mandatory sentencing.[33] As presented in Chapter 3, juvenile waiver laws were expanded, prosecutors were given increased powers to charge juveniles in adult court, and reforms that had been embraced 10 years earlier were replaced by a system stressing accountability, punishment, and incapacitation. Harsher alternative sanctions also were adopted, including intensive supervision and electronic monitoring. Also, the highly confrontational Scared Straight program, which involved adult prison inmates "scaring" delinquents and at-risk youths into a life of law-abiding behavior, became a popular (but ineffective) prevention and early intervention strategy. Finally, new conclusions that juvenile correctional treatment programs were having little positive impact on recidivism[34] convinced all but the most ardent supporters of the rehabilitative ideal that getting tough was the best way to go.

Youth Violence, Punishment, and Rehabilitation

Interestingly, just as the get tough philosophy was being adopted in juvenile justice, youth violence began what turned out to be a 10-year climb that did not end until the mid-1990s. Rather than this causing a reconsideration of the "punish and incarcerate" approach, legislative efforts accelerated to increase accountability, reduce confidentiality, and strengthen sanctions in juvenile court.[35] Transferring greater numbers of serious and violent offenders to adult court became a top priority, despite the lack of scientific evidence to support this practice.[36] By 1995, at the height of the superpredator panic, it appeared to many that the only thing that could save society was the further punishment and incarceration of morally depraved youths who were violently taking over the nation's streets.[37]

Unfortunately, what was not being discussed openly were the research findings being produced regarding the causes and treatment of serious, violent, and chronic juvenile delinquency. Several books, large-scale reviews of modern research, and meta-analyses of earlier studies were published that revealed relationships between risk factors, protective factors, and delinquent behavior as well as evidence of effectiveness for a variety of prevention, early intervention, and rehabilitation programs being offered to at-risk children and known delinquents.[38] Essentially, juvenile justice was being revived in a way that emphasized doing things differently from the crackdown and get tough approaches.

Overall, during the past decade, those in the field of juvenile justice and delinquency prevention have stressed the stronger use of scientific research; reducing risk factors and enhancing protective factors in families, schools, communities, and within children and youths; providing treatment and rehabilitation programs that focus on risk and needs assessment; matching high-risk youths and offenders with structured services to improve behavioral and social skills; and supplying well-designed community-based programs, smaller and more treatment-oriented correctional facilities, and enriched aftercare services. Much scientific evidence exists to support these practices, and at the same time that these approaches have been taken, delinquency and youth violence have declined to levels representative of the early 1980s (that is, the start of the get tough movement in juvenile justice).[39]

CORRECTIONAL EXPERIENCES OF INCARCERATED YOUTHS

The use of incarceration remains the primary method of responding to more frequent, serious, and violent youthful offenders despite a recent reemergence of rehabilitation in American correctional systems and a corresponding emphasis on prevention, early intervention, and research-based treatment in juvenile justice. On any given day, more than 100,000 juveniles younger than 18 are housed in residential correctional facilities, and roughly 15,000 of these youths are incarcerated in adult jails and prisons.[40] They are predominantly male, and most are minorities, as disproportionate minority confinement is characteristic of both the juvenile and adult systems. In this section, we will turn our attention to the conditions and programming offered to young offenders in both juvenile and adult facilities.

Juvenile Secure Corrections

Nationally, more than 350 youths are in juvenile secure custody for every 100,000 in the population.[41] Only about one third are violent or person offenders, and more than half have been convicted of property or public order offenses. Person offenders do appear to experience longer periods of confinement than other juveniles, but the average incarceration time also varies by facility type and placement status. On average, juveniles committed to public residential facilities undergo lengthier incarceration periods than do youths committed to private facilities. However, for offenders housed in shorter-term detention centers, those in private facilities tend to experience longer incarceration periods than their counterparts in public centers.

During the get tough movement of the 1980s and 1990s, overcrowding became an increasing problem in many juvenile detention and residential correctional facilities.[42] At the end of the century, approximately 70% of youths in public facilities were housed in buildings operating at more than their design capacity, and a similar percentage were contained in locked rather than staff-secure settings. These figures run counter to the goal of national accreditation standards, which emphasize the placement of juveniles in the least restrictive placement alternative possible. Moreover, based on reports of tens of thousands of injuries sustained annually by adolescents as a result of staff or inmate violence, some have concluded that "the daily reality of juveniles confined in many 'treatment' facilities is one of violence, predatory behavior, and punitive incarceration."[43]

Despite these facts, figures, and less-than-supportive conclusions about the conditions in many juvenile facilities, there also is reliable evidence available indicating that juvenile correctional programming can effectively treat serious and violent young offenders.[44] For example, since the early 1990s, Mark Lipsey has been conducting and reporting on large-scale meta-analyses of juvenile treatment programs, which allows for the systematic and statistical summarization of program evaluation results.[45] His initial findings, based on nearly 400 studies, revealed that juveniles in treatment groups exhibited recidivism rates about 10% lower than those of untreated youths, and the most effective programs produced up to a 37% reduction in recidivism. His more recent work has focused on the treatment of serious and violent juvenile offenders, where, on the basis of 200 studies, he found an average recidivism reduction of 12%. More effective programs, however, were found capable of reducing recidivism by as much as 40%.

Lipsey's results also indicated that treatment effects for serious and violent youthful offenders were similar for those in both institutional (secure) and noninstitutional programs. Furthermore, interventions typically were more effective for more serious offenders than for less serious offenders, and program characteristics emerged as the strongest predictor of treatment effectiveness for the institutionalized youths. Overall, institutional programs that were found to produce the largest treatment effects were those focused on building interpersonal skills and providing cognitive-behavioral training, and those offered in smaller, community-based residential settings and supplying multiple services.

These findings are supported by other studies done during the same time period that suggest that rehabilitation can work if programs target higher-risk offenders as well as crime-producing factors and needs that can be changed. The findings also suggest that, to be effective programs should deliver styles and modes of treatment that match the learning styles and abilities of the participating offenders (generally following a cognitive-behavioral or social learning approach).[46] If treatment and rehabilitation programs can produce positive behavioral change, the question then becomes: Which system can provide the best opportunity and setting for these programs? Although there certainly is evidence that some juvenile correctional facilities present substandard conditions and less than adequate services, studies to date also suggest that what typically is offered to juveniles in adult facilities does not rise to even that level.

Adult Secure Corrections for Juveniles

As revealed in the previous chapter, many serious and violent juvenile offenders who are convicted in criminal court do serve sentences of incarceration. Based on a nationwide survey of adult jails and prisons, James Austin and colleagues determined that in 1998, 44 states housed juveniles (age 17 and younger) in adult correctional facilities.[47] Of the approximate 14,500 youths in adult custody at that time, 21% were held as adjudicated juveniles or pretrial detainees, while 75% had been sentenced as adults. Moreover, of the 44 state prison systems housing juveniles as adults, only 18 were maintaining designated youthful offender housing units, and just 13% of the 181 total facilities surveyed were doing so. These findings suggest that juveniles tried in adult court and sentenced to incarceration really are likely to serve adult time.

As discussed by Donna Bishop, juvenile and adult institutions are different in several fundamental ways.[48] First, prison populations are much older, on average, than juvenile facility populations. Roughly half of all prison inmates are in their mid-20s to mid-30s, while nearly three quarters of all youths in juvenile institutions are ages 15 to 17. Older offender ages are correlated with greater size and physical strength, longer and more violent criminal histories, and more experience with incarceration, meaning transferred and incarcerated youths are exposed to a different type of inmate than typically exists in juvenile institutions. This exposure also commonly takes place during an extended period of time.

Second, juvenile and adult facilities exhibit organizational differences. Adult institutions tend to be much larger, often holding between 500 and 1,000 inmates, or about 10 times the average of juvenile facilities. Although overcrowding and disproportionate minority confinement are concerns in both juvenile and adult institutions, these problems are at least slightly more pronounced in jails and prisons. Institutional size and overcrowding have been linked to levels of facility violence and other adverse consequences, and contemporary treatment and rehabilitation research indicates that smaller and more structured facilities can provide more effective services (particularly those facilities operating in the juvenile system).[49]

Third, staffing patterns are markedly different between juvenile and adult institutions.[50] Jails and prisons generally place a high priority on security and custody, with a majority of personnel hired to address concerns in these areas. Moreover, in custody-oriented facilities, inmate perceptions of oppression, alienation, and danger have a tendency to be higher. On the other hand, staffing for education and treatment programs is given greater priority in juvenile facilities, where inmate-to-staff ratios are much more favorable than in adult institutions. In addition, in more treatment-oriented facilities, relationships with staff and other inmates tend to be more positive, and inmates are more receptive to the idea of change and remaining law abiding upon release.

Whether these differences in population age, organizational structure, and staff composition translate into serious problems for youths in jails and prisons is an important question to consider. Unfortunately, available evidence does not suggest a very pleasant answer. Although research on this topic is limited, several studies show that compared with offenders placed in juvenile institutions, youths in adult facilities are far more likely to be sexually assaulted, attacked by inmates, beaten by staff, perceive unfair treatment, and commit suicide.[51] Other corrections research indicates that younger inmates who lack the experience to deal with the prison environment are at the greatest risk for physical and sexual assault and exhibit the greatest fear and vulnerability.[52] Also, recent studies show that correctional administrators have serious concerns regarding the placement of juveniles in adult correctional facilities and about what the adult system does and does not offer these youths.[53] These studies also indicate that many adult institutions are ill-equipped to handle juveniles and to provide the specialized programming and services that are typically provided in the juvenile system.[54]

As asserted by juvenile justice scholar Richard Redding, "it is hard to imagine how the conditions and criminal culture of adult prisons could be rehabilitative for juvenile offenders."[55] However, in response to this state of affairs, several state correctional systems have developed specialized programming and behavioral management techniques to deal with incarcerated juvenile offenders.[56] In these relatively few states, judges may be given more discretion to impose indeterminate sentences on transferred youths, juveniles can be housed separately from adult inmates, and a wider variety of treatment programs and therapeutic environments exist. However, practices like these represent the exception, rather than the norm, for the processing and handling of youths incarcerated in adult jails and prisons. Moreover, as illustrated recently in Pennsylvania, specialized efforts to handle juveniles in adult facilities do not always work as anticipated.

THE PINE GROVE STATE CORRECTIONAL INSTITUTION

As discussed in Chapter 3, in the mid-1990s, Pennsylvania fell in line with the nationwide trend to pass legislation that sought to facilitate the transfer of serious and violent juvenile offenders to adult criminal court. In response to rising levels of youth violence and growing fear of future superpredators, Act 33 statutorily excluded specified youths from juvenile court jurisdiction and enabled those offenders to be prosecuted as adults from the time of arrest. Because initial estimates indicated that this legislation would contribute an additional 500 prisoners to the state's prison population and perhaps as a result of concerns about housing juveniles with adult prison inmates, $52 million was authorized for construction of a separate facility to incarcerate this new population.[57]

The Pine Grove State Correctional Institution (SCI Pine Grove) subsequently was built in western Pennsylvania and was proposed to be unique in several ways.[58] First, it was to be one of the initial adult-style facilities in the country devoted to juveniles tried and sentenced in adult court. Second, education and behavioral modification services were to be offered in a highly structured, therapeutic-community environment. Finally, the prison was to include a strong research emphasis and presence in an effort to link research and practice and to create scientific knowledge about violent youthful offenders and promising strategies for changing their behavior. In general, the planned approach for the institution was consistent with much of the contemporary research on treatment and rehabilitation.

A number of things are now worth noting about SCI Pine Grove. To begin, at an actual cost of over $70 million, the facility did not open until January 2001, nearly five years after Pennsylvania's legislative waiver law went into effect. This exemplifies how policies are often passed without the proper planning and resources in place for them to be effective. Next, the influx of juvenile inmates that was expected did not materialize. After operating for several months at roughly 33% of the total capacity, the prison began accepting adult inmates from the rest of the state system to fill bed space and reduce overcrowding in other prisons.[59] This produced an adult to juvenile inmate ratio of 2 to 1 as well as concerns among policymakers about cost (an estimated $53,000 per inmate) and overall effectiveness of the facility. Finally, originally planned research efforts stalled soon after the institution was opened, and little or no meaningful evaluation evidence has been produced that would provide an indication of the value of this facility in housing and treating violent youthful offenders.

Since 1996, when Act 33 went into effect, the Pennsylvania Department of Corrections has never received more than 97 inmates under the age of 18 in any given year.[60] From 1999 through 2002, fewer than 50 juvenile offenders were committed each year to the state's adult correctional system; these figures are virtually identical to those of the early to mid-1990s. Furthermore, committed inmates younger than 18 represent only 0.1% of the population of inmates housed in Pennsylvania state prisons. The basic reason, then, that SCI Pine Grove did not fill up with violent youthful offenders is that not very many have received a state prison sentence (which requires at least a two-year sentence in Pennsylvania).

There are several likely reasons for the unexpected low number of juveniles sent to state prison in Pennsylvania since the enactment of Act 33. Perhaps most importantly, it appears that corrections officials and other policymakers underestimated how many offenders originally excluded from juvenile court under the new law later would be decertified back to juvenile court or would have their charges dismissed in adult court. As discussed in Chapter 4, studies by S. I. Singer and, in Pennsylvania, by Snyder and colleagues suggest that about 75% of all youths legislatively waived to adult court either get decertified or have their charges dismissed, meaning only 25% are convicted in adult court.[61] This is an area in need of further research, but few would have anticipated figures like these following the enactment of Act 33.

In addition, similar to the rest of the nation, Pennsylvania experienced a sharp decline in youth violence since the mid-1990s.[62] Rather than the onslaught of juvenile superpredators that was expected, fewer violent youths entered the system, meaning fewer were available by the time of sentencing for placement in SCI Pine Grove. Last, in light of research findings, their own perceptions, or both, adult court judges appear reluctant to send all but the most serious and violent youthful offenders to state prison. In the study by Snyder and colleagues, only about half of the roughly 100 Pennsylvania youths actually convicted in adult court under Act 33 subsequently received state prison sentences.[63] These findings correspond well with the fact that there were only 51 court commitments to the Pennsylvania Department of Corrections in 1996.[64] To the extent that shorter terms of incarceration are imposed in an effort to keep juveniles in a county facility, the level of educational and treatment services available in county jails and prisons could be cause for concern.

SUMMARY AND CONCLUSIONS

Since the late 1960s, both the adult and juvenile justice systems in America have swung from a rehabilitative orientation to a punishment-oriented philosophy focused on retribution, incapacitation, and deterrence.

The adult criminal justice system led this charge in the early 1970s, but by the late 1970s and early 1980s, the juvenile system had followed along. As youth violence increased from the mid-1980s to the mid-1990s, calls for getting tough with serious and violent young offenders intensified, fueling the modern transfer movement. Operating in the background, though, were correctional rehabilitation programs that have been supported by research for both juveniles and adults. In particular, contemporary studies have produced a great deal of knowledge regarding risk factors, protective factors, and problem juvenile behavior, and strong evidence exists concerning the effectiveness of a variety of prevention, early intervention, and juvenile rehabilitation programs.

Research also indicates that although some juvenile correctional facilities do not offer suitable programs and living conditions, effective treatment services can be provided to institutionalized youths that do result in lowered recidivism. Furthermore, studies of juveniles housed in adult jails and prisons paint a grim picture of overcrowded and understaffed surroundings, victimization of youths by older inmates and staff, and an emphasis on custody and security rather than treatment and rehabilitation. It also appears that most adult institutions simply are not prepared to handle adolescent offenders, and most jails and prisons treat these youths like other adult inmates. Finally, even when unique efforts have been made to incarcerate juveniles in specialized adult prisons such as SCI Pine Grove, unexpected results have been seen that weaken support for these practices.

Overall, the evidence suggests that effective treatment and rehabilitation can be provided to serious and violent youthful offenders and that the juvenile system generally provides a better chance for positive behavioral change. However, another question pertaining to the effectiveness of trying and sentencing juveniles as adults involves the deterrent effects of formal sanctions, including those provided through waiver policies and practices. In other words, do stronger punishments in general and expanded transfer laws specifically result in less juvenile crime (as a result of the threat of harsher punishment in adult court), and are punished youths and those who are waived less likely to commit crime in the future as a result of these experiences?

CHAPTER 7

General and Specific Deterrence

During the past 30 years, policymakers generally have reacted to public concerns and fear of crime by supporting various get tough strategies. The more popular approaches have included "three strikes and you're out" laws, "truth in sentencing" provisions, expanded use of the death penalty, boot camps, and stricter law enforcement. While these measures often are backed with a belief in the value of increased retribution and incapacitation, they also are supported based on the idea that punishment deters criminal and delinquent behavior. Moreover, this stance is very appealing to the general public. Not only is it assumed that formal punishments have a deterrent effect but also that harsher sanctions are needed. As noted by James Q. Wilson, "Despite their good instincts for the right answers, the people, frustrated by the restraints (many wise, some foolish) on swiftness and certainty, vote for proposals to increase severity: if the penalty is ten years, let us make it twenty or thirty; if the penalty is life imprisonment, let us make it death; if the penalty is jail, let us make it caning."[1]

Transferring juveniles to adult criminal court corresponds well with this view. Supporters of this practice contend that adult court is the appropriate place for youthful offenders who exhibit serious and violent criminal behavior. It is asserted that in adult court a message can be sent that the lenient treatment of the juvenile system is no longer an option.[2]

Instead, harsh criminal court sanctions will be imposed, which will increase public safety and reduce motivations to commit future crimes. In sum, adult criminal court is believed to provide stronger punishment and greater deterrence.

These underlying beliefs suggest that the effectiveness of treating juvenile offenders as adults is based on the nature of the punishment it produces (that is, the certainty, severity, and swiftness of the punishment) and subsequent criminal behavior.[3] Considering the deterrent effects of formal sanctions by reviewing the origins of deterrence theory and considering how researchers have assessed its central components is essential to understanding the issues. Reviewing the deterrent effects of transferring juveniles to adult court reveals that the expected deterrent effects from juvenile transfer frequently are often unrealized.

ORIGINS OF DETERRENCE THEORY

Deterrence theory can be traced to the development of the classical school of criminology in the latter half of the eighteenth century. According to classical criminology, humans are rational beings who are guided by their own free will. Therefore, both criminal and law-abiding behavior results from conscious choice. Based on this underlying belief, Cesare Beccaria proposed a more rational system of justice in his influential work, *On Crimes and Punishments*.[4] In reaction to the often arbitrary and cruel systems of justice that were in place during the 1700s, Beccaria presented a series of criminal justice reforms. His proposals covered such topics as making laws public and simple to understand, eliminating the torture of suspects, a presumption of innocence until proven guilty, equality under the law, and abolishing the death penalty. Furthermore, he stressed that the key purpose of punishment should be deterrence and that to achieve maximum deterrence, punishment should be based on the principles of certainty, severity, and swiftness.

Although the swiftness, or celerity, of punishment generally has been ignored in modern deterrence research, Beccaria placed great emphasis on it:

> The more prompt the punishment is and the sooner it follows the crime, the more just and useful it will be. I say more just, because it spares the criminal the useless and cruel torments of uncertainty.... I have said that

promptness of punishment is more useful, for the less time that passes between the misdeed and its chastisement, the stronger and more permanent is the human mind's association of the two ideas of crime and punishment, so that imperceptibly the one will come to be considered as the cause and the other as the necessary and inevitable result.[5]

In addition to the importance of swift punishments, Beccaria also stressed the need for punishments to be a certain response to criminal behavior:

One of the greatest checks on crime is not the cruelty of punishments but their inevitability.... The certainty of a chastisement, even if it be moderate, will always make a greater impression than the fear of a more terrible punishment that is united with the hope of impunity; for, when they are certain, even the least of evils always terrifies men's minds, while hope, that heavenly gift that often fills us completely, always removes from us the idea of worse punishments, especially if that hope is reinforced by the examples of impunity which weakness and greed frequently accord.[6]

Finally, while addressing the importance of certain punishments, Beccaria also cautioned against punishments that were too severe:

The very savagery of a punishment makes the criminal all the bolder in taking risks to avoid it precisely because the evil with which he is threatened is so great, so much so that he commits several crimes in order to escape the punishment for a single one of them.... In order for a penalty to achieve its objective, all that is required is that the harm of the punishment should exceed the benefit resulting from the crime.... Everything more than this is thus superfluous and therefore tyrannical.[7]

These three principles of punishment continue to receive attention today from criminologists, politicians, and the general public. However, contemporary scholars have emphasized the certainty and, to a lesser extent, the severity of punishment, while the swiftness of punishment has received little consideration.[8] Citizens and politicians tend to be even more narrowly focused, placing their support squarely behind those policies that promise the harshest punishment.[9] Interestingly, this emphasis on severe punishment directly contradicts the original writings of Beccaria. Furthermore, considering what is known from research about the deterrent effects of formal sanctions, policies that focus mainly on increasing the severity of punishment appear to be the most questionable.

DETERRENCE RESEARCH

Although deterrence theory is more than 200 years old, its propositions have been tested empirically only during the past few decades.[10] Throughout this time, researchers have distinguished between two types of deterrence, both of which originally were suggested by Beccaria.[11] First, specific, or special, deterrence pertains to the effect of punishment on the behavior of the individual who is sanctioned. In other words, when someone is deterred in the future by the actual experience of punishment, this constitutes specific deterrence.[12] In contrast, general deterrence refers to the effect of punishment on potential offenders in the greater community or an instance in which sanctions are imposed on one person in order to demonstrate to everyone else the expected costs of crime and thereby discourage criminal behavior among the general population.[13] Overall, specific deterrence has been thought to impact offenders who have been caught and punished, while general deterrence has been applied to those in the general public who have not yet offended or experienced punishment.

General Deterrence

Research on deterrence theory usually is classified according to one type of deterrence or the other, with most involving general rather than specific deterrence.[14] Earlier studies focused on exploring the relationship between cumulative, or aggregate, levels of risk and officially recorded crime rates. In these cases, researchers examined the associations between state-level measures of arrest rates and incarceration rates (certainty of punishment), average lengths of incarceration (severity of punishment), and officially recorded crime rates.[15] These studies found inconsistent support for general deterrence (that is, inconsistent evidence of an inverse relationship between the certainty and severity of punishment and aggregate crime rates), but it did appear that the certainty of punishment had a larger general deterrent effect than punishment severity.[16]

Subsequent researchers soon discussed the possibility that general deterrence could depend more on individual perceptions of the certainty and severity of punishment rather than aggregate or overall levels of punishment certainty and severity. This recognition of deterrence as a perceptual theory has guided much of the modern deterrence research. By the early 1980s, numerous studies revealed a moderately strong inverse relationship between perceptions of certain punishment and various criminal behaviors.[17] These same studies generally failed to find a similar inverse association between the perceived severity of punishment and illegal acts.

In addition, other researchers demonstrated with longitudinal data (that is, data collected during a period of time) that active participants in crime often do not get caught, which actually leads to lower estimates of punishment risk.[18] This means that earlier perceptual studies actually were measuring an experiential effect of prior behavior on current perceptions of risk rather than a true deterrent effect of perceived risk on behavior. When the experiential and true deterrent effects were separated using longitudinal data, a much weaker deterrent effect from perceived certainty of punishment was found than earlier research had indicated. Furthermore, longitudinal studies that also controlled for greater numbers of other explanatory factors found the least evidence of a deterrent effect from the perceived risk of formal sanctions.[19]

By the mid-1980s, research on general deterrence indicated relatively little reason to be optimistic about the beneficial effects of formal sanctions. However, longitudinal studies also had revealed that individual perceptions of risk were unstable, often varying significantly from time to time.[20] This finding led to a major improvement in more recent research, resulting in conclusions that are more supportive of the presence of general deterrence. During the past 15 years, researchers have used scenarios to elicit perceptions of the risk of punishment and behavioral intentions to commit crime at the same time. This method permits respondents to consider detailed information regarding the circumstances of proposed criminal behavior, allowing for a more-informed response to questions of sanction risk and projected behavior.[21] The use of scenarios also overcomes the problems of experiential effects and instability of risk perceptions that plagued earlier studies.

With these improvements, modern research has demonstrated that perceived threats of punishment do operate as a deterrent, at least for some people.[22] While controlling for such factors as potential rewards, moral beliefs, informal sanctions, peer delinquency, possible victim reaction, and low self-control, perceived sanction risk has been found to have a significant deterrent effect on a variety of criminal behaviors.[23] Furthermore, a number of other studies have assessed the general deterrent effects of various criminal justice policies and programs (for example, police crackdowns and mandatory sentencing) and have found supportive evidence.[24] Overall, contemporary research has shown that earlier research, which suffered from methodological problems and often failed to find supportive evidence, might have been premature in dismissing the general deterrent effect of formal sanctions, especially with regard to the perceived certainty of punishment.

Specific Deterrence

While a great deal of research has investigated the general deterrent effect of formal sanctions, other studies have considered how personal experiences with punishment affect future criminal behavior. Specific deterrence, in its simplest form, occurs when individuals who have experienced a punishment refrain from committing crime in the future because of the fear of further punishment.[25] This process can be expanded to include not only a cessation in offending but also a reduction in the seriousness of offenses committed or in the rate at which they take place.[26] From this perspective, individuals who experience a more certain, swift, and severe punishment will be more likely to reduce or refrain from future offending than those who are punished with less certainty, severity, and swiftness.[27]

Unfortunately, the question of how legal punishments actually affect future individual behavior is not an easy one to answer. An enduring debate in the field of criminology concerns whether formal sanctions reduce or amplify future criminal offending.[28] Deterrence theory has been opposed by labeling theory, which argues that legal punishments can increase, rather than reduce, future offending among those sanctioned.[29] This increase in criminal behavior may be a result of diminished opportunities for success in legitimate activities, or it may be caused by a process of self-identification and value development in which the individual who is "labeled" adopts the norms and behavior patterns that are characteristic of the label.[30] In any case, the fundamental prediction of labeling theory is that being punished or negatively labeled will increase one's involvement in future deviant conduct, which is referred to as a deviance-amplification effect.[31]

While studying the effects of legal sanctions requires recognition of two contradicting theoretical predictions, the task is made even more difficult by the potential obstacle of selection bias. To illustrate, a simple test of whether formal punishments have any effect on subsequent criminal behavior could involve comparisons of future offending across groups whose members naturally received different court dispositions. However, this design is problematic, as "assignment to treatment groups (diversion vs. referred to juvenile court, for example) is the result of a nonrandom process in which high-risk youths are more likely to receive severe dispositions. Thus, those individuals assigned more severe sanctions would be more likely to commit new offenses whether any relationship existed between juvenile court dispositions and future offending."[32]

The difficulty of selection bias can be approached in various fashions. In conjunction with large samples, the ideal way to assure the comparability of treatment and control groups is to use random assignment of subjects into these groups.[33] Unfortunately, this is often difficult or not always possible in justice system research (for example, in studying juvenile transfer to adult court). Therefore, other methods have been employed, although the danger of selection bias remains. One strategy is to use a matching design, whereby the subjects in treatment and control groups are matched on the basis of specified variables. The major problem with this method is obtaining large groups matched on more than a few relevant variables.[34] An alternative and more often used strategy is to obtain statistical control of possible explanatory variables by using multivariate statistical models. The remaining difficulty here is the possible omission of any variables that influence both the probability of formal sanctions being imposed and the likelihood of future offending (for example, variables pertaining to offending history). In sum, the following research on the specific deterrent effects of formal sanctions needs to be interpreted with caution.[35]

Arresting Youthful Offenders

An early study on this topic was conducted by Gold and Williams.[36] Using 35 matched pairs of juveniles who self-reported their delinquent activity, the authors tested the proposition that youths who are apprehended by police for an offense will have more subsequent offenses than comparable youths who are not apprehended. In 57% of the pairs, the apprehended youths reported more subsequent delinquency than the unapprehended youths (that is, a deviance amplification effect). In 29% of the pairs, the apprehended youths committed fewer offenses (that is, a specific deterrent effect). In the remaining 14% of the pairs, the two juveniles committed an equal number of offenses.

Gold and Williams argued that these results support the hypothesis derived from labeling theory. However, their study presents various methodological weaknesses. Most obvious is the small number of matched pairs, which points to the difficulty in matching groups on the basis of several criteria. A total of 74 apprehended youths had been originally selected for the study, but it was possible to match only 35 with unapprehended juveniles. Furthermore, there was a lack of any control for the seriousness of reported prior offenses, which raises doubt about the similarity of the matched offenders. Overall, this study provides weak support for the argument that formal sanctions increase future delinquent behavior.

Subsequent research by L. W. Klemke, however, produced similar findings.[37] Self-report data on shoplifting were collected from 1,189 high school students in the Pacific Northwest. The ensuing analysis revealed that apprehension by store personnel and by parents was directly related to future shoplifting activity and the identification of oneself as a "troublemaker," as predicted by labeling theory. In addition, subsequent shoplifting and adoption of a deviant self-concept were much more strongly related to parental apprehension than to apprehension by store personnel. Finally, youths who experienced police intervention exhibited greater subsequent shoplifting than those who did not go through police involvement. However, this study also employed a weak control for prior delinquency (a measure only of recent shoplifting), which allows for the possibility that apprehended youths and those exposed to the police were simply more serious delinquents.

A later study by Smith and Gartin improved upon the efforts of Gold and Williams and Klemke.[38] Using data on police contacts for all males born in Racine, Wisconsin, in 1949 and followed until age 25, the authors examined the influence of arrest on four different dimensions of subsequent criminal behavior: termination from future criminal behavior, future offending rate, duration of the future offending period, and time until next offense. The final sample consisted of 325 males who had at least one recorded police contact for a misdemeanor or felony.

Contrary to earlier research, Smith and Gartin uncovered evidence that supported a specific deterrence effect. With controls for the seriousness of the current offense and the extent of prior offending, being arrested was found to affect specific aspects of a criminal career differently. The combined effect was a reduction in future criminal behavior among those offenders who were arrested relative to those who were contacted by police but not arrested. Being arrested was associated with an increased probability of desistance among novice offenders, but as offenders acquired more police contacts, this effect of arrest on future police contacts diminished. Still, arrest was consistently related to reduced rates of future police contacts, and this finding became more pronounced as criminal careers persisted. Furthermore, for those offenders who persisted in their criminal behavior, arrest appeared to not only extend the duration of their criminal career but to also increase the time until next police contact. Finally, arrest was found to have a negative effect on the total number of future police contacts.

Smith and Gartin's research provided evidence of a specific deterrent effect resulting from formal sanctions. Their study was stronger than earlier works, with better controls for offense seriousness and prior offending and a comprehensive examination of future criminal activity. However, the measurement of criminal behavior was based solely on official records of police contacts, which underestimate true rates of offending. Also, official records were used to select a rather small sample of known offenders. A larger sample would have permitted the authors "to disaggregate police contacts by offense type and estimate models separately for different types of crimes or for felonies relative to misdemeanors."[39] Finally, the degree of actual punishment associated with arrest could have varied greatly among offenders because many cases might have been subsequently dismissed by prosecutors. Thus, while support for a specific deterrent effect from legal punishment was presented, several avenues remained open for further investigation.

A more recent study by Paternoster and Piquero illustrates this point.[40] Based on self-reported data obtained from more than 1,400 high school students from nine schools in and around a southeastern city, the authors tested a reconceptualization of deterrence presented by Stafford and Warr.[41] In doing so, they examined the effect of both personal experience with punishment and punishment avoidance, and vicarious experience with punishment and punishment avoidance. Central to the current discussion, the authors found that those youths who reported past experience with being apprehended by police, taken to a police station, arrested, or taken to juvenile court were more likely to drink alcohol and use marijuana in the future than those who were not legally punished. The significant positive effect from formal sanctions remained even when the number of previous delinquent acts was controlled.

Punishing Youthful Offenders

While the research discussed to this point focused on the future offending of juveniles who were apprehended relative to those who were not, other studies have looked at the effects of varying degrees of punishment on known offenders. In the much debated and somewhat controversial Provo Experiment, delinquent boys in Utah were randomly assigned to experimental and control groups.[42] The experimental intervention was community-based and provided intensive treatment services. Comparisons were made with a randomly selected group that had been placed on regular probation as well as a matched group that was institutionalized in a training school. The effectiveness of the treatment program was evaluated based on arrests both during program participation and after the treatment had ended.

The authors reported that boys in the community-based program were significantly less delinquent while under supervision than those placed on regular probation and that they were no more delinquent than youths in the training school. Juveniles in the latter group committed as much delinquency while home on short furloughs or following escape as did the experimental group that was free in the community. An analysis of post-program recidivism revealed little difference between the experimental and control groups. However, when preprogram arrests were compared with postprogram arrests, the results supported both the community program and institutionalization as an effective deterrent to offending. Arrests were reduced by 25% for those juveniles who were institutionalized and by 70% for those who remained free in the community.

Although these findings seem to support a deterrent, rehabilitative, or combined effect from correctional programs and in doing so contradict the conclusion that "nothing works," they also need to be treated with caution. The reductions in arrests following correctional intervention could have been a result of natural maturation on the part of the juveniles or because their delinquent behavior peaked just before the sanction was imposed and then declined to a normal level.[43] Other potential problems with the Provo Experiment include selection bias, the reliance on official arrest data to measure recidivism, and a relatively short follow-up period that could create an illusory deterrent effect.[44]

Unfortunately, these same criticisms can be applied to a later study that produced somewhat similar findings. Murray and Cox examined chronic delinquents in Chicago who were either incarcerated in a state reformatory or were diverted to one of several less-custodial community-based programs.[45] Although all of the youths had lengthy records of delinquency, those who were chosen for the community programs were presumed to be somewhat less dangerous and perhaps more amenable to treatment. However, the study produced several striking outcomes that would appear to support a deterrent effect from increasingly severe formal sanctions.

A comparison of preprogram and postprogram delinquent behavior revealed a larger reduction in offending among youths sent to reformatories relative to those who remained in the community. Additionally, for youths who remained in the community, the greatest reduction in arrests occurred among those who experienced the most restrictive forms of supervision. Murray and Cox suggested that these findings indicate evidence of a suppression effect from increasingly restrictive sanctions and that court-mandated intervention is the most effective deterrent to chronic juvenile offending. However, as with the Provo Experiment, their conclusions can be challenged on the grounds of subject maturation and the issue of whether the decline in official arrests represents a decrease in criminal behavior or an increase in ability to avoid apprehension.

Subsequent researchers studying the effects of varying levels of formal punishment sought to improve upon earlier works. For example, M. W. Klein randomly assigned 306 juvenile arrestees, all initially considered referable for further processing, to four different conditions: release, referral to a social service program, referral to a social service program with purchase of treatment, and formal petition for prosecution.[46] By the end of a six-month follow-up period, a trend had emerged that as the level of case processing increased, so did the chances of rearrest. This trend continued through a 27-month follow-up period, with released offenders rearrested less commonly than all others and petitioned offenders rearrested most commonly. In the middle, there was a widening gap between the two social service conditions. The purchase of treatment condition, which provided compensated rehabilitative programming for the youth and was expected to ensure higher quality treatment services, actually yielded an increasingly greater number of arrests.

In general, Klein's findings on rearrests indicated that diversion to a community agency was less harmful than petitioning to juvenile court but more harmful than outright release. However, no similar differences emerged in terms of self-reported delinquent behavior. This could be because only 185 of the original 306 subjects referred for random assignment were subsequently interviewed regarding their future offending. A higher interview rate might have confirmed the findings from the official data. On the other hand, the results concerning rearrests could be a result of police selection bias. Klein reported that there were attempts made by police officers to circumvent the randomization process. This allows for the possibility that youths perceived as less serious offenders received a lower level of formal processing. In addition, juveniles perceived as more serious offenders might have received a higher level of formal processing and police may also have targeted them for rearrest.

In a subsequent study of the same issue, Wooldredge examined the relative effectiveness of 12 different juvenile court dispositions on eliminating recidivism among 2,038 youthful offenders in Illinois.[47] Court actions ranged from case dismissals to incarceration with a variety of combinations employed. Recidivism was measured based on future juvenile and adult arrests during a follow-up period of three to seven years, and several multivariate analyses were conducted. While controlling for a wide range of individual and environmental characteristics, a combination of probation supervision and community treatment was found to be associated with the least recidivism. Contrary to the findings of Klein, eight of 11 dispositional options yielded lower recidivism rates than the case dismissal option. Shorter terms of supervision and longer terms of community treatment were found to be effective in eliminating and prolonging recidivism, while longer terms of incarceration were found to be counterproductive. Based on these results, Wooldredge concluded:

> While it appears that "doing something" is better than "doing nothing" for eliminating recidivism, this study suggests that differences in "something" may also yield differences in recidivism rates. Specifically, two

years of court supervision with community treatment is superior to any other sentence examined in this study for eliminating and prolonging recidivism. On the other hand, sentences involving detention should be carefully considered in relation to the types of delinquents they may be effective on. Failure to make such considerations could serve to inflate aggregate recidivism rates.... While such sentencing may be inconsequential for specific deterrence in some cases, it can actually be damaging in others.[48]

Building on the work of Klein and Wooldredge, Schneider and Ervin used in-person interviews and official records of 876 adjudicated delinquents from six cities to examine intentions of engaging in delinquent activity (measured at time 1) and subsequent offenses during a two- to three-year follow-up period (time 2).[49] The sample over-represented serious and chronic juvenile offenders, or those "for whom general deterrence has already proven to be ineffective" and at whom "crime control policies are directed."

Through pooling the data from the six juvenile courts, the authors found that the dispositional options of incarceration and regular probation produced significantly greater recidivism than the option of restitution. Furthermore, youths who had been punished more severely, as indicated by the number of days incarcerated, reported being less certain of getting caught and committed more, rather than fewer, subsequent crimes. Although the results varied somewhat by city, Schneider and Ervin concluded that "the results from this study clearly suggest that punishment-oriented policies may set in motion unintended effects on self-image or other values that culminated in more crimes being committed. Yet, many public officials and many social scientists are confident that increases in the severity or certainty of punishment will reduce crime."[50]

A study by Gottfredson and Barton would appear, at least at first glance, to contradict the findings of Klein, Wooldredge, and Schneider and Ervin.[51] Here, the researchers investigated the effects of the 1988 closing of the Montrose Training School in Maryland. A group of 673 youths who had been incarcerated in the institution was compared with a group of 254 youths who had a high statistical probability of being institutionalized, but juveniles in the latter group did not go to Montrose because they were referred to the Department of Juvenile Services after admissions to the facility had ceased. These youths spent little or no time in any other institution and were instead placed in community-based programs. Recidivism was measured through both official records and face-to-face interviews, although only 750 interviews were attempted and the overall response rate was 62.5%.

Gottfredson and Barton found that during a two-and-a-half-year follow-up period, the incarcerated juveniles had significantly fewer arrests than the noninstitutionalized youths, but the difference was less substantial when only serious offenses were considered. Furthermore, the results from the self-reports of criminal behavior did not show the same degree of differential recidivism that was indicated by official records. This was possibly the result of a number of factors including a longer follow-up period for interviews relative to the examination of official records; youths who were interviewed being more delinquent than those who were not, which could diminish group differences; or the inclusion of relatively minor crimes in the self-reports. Nevertheless, the results indicated that recidivism was greater among youths in the community-based programs than among those who were incarcerated, which would imply a greater deterrent, rehabilitative, or combined effect from the more restrictive sanction.

However, this conclusion should be treated with caution. The study was conducted immediately after the closing of the institution, when the community programs were at the earliest stages of implementation. As noted by Gottfredson and Barton, their findings suggest "that the alternatives available when Montrose was closed were less effective in reducing crime than institutionalization would have been."[52] It may be that if the less restrictive programs had been operating for a longer period of time, the quality of services provided would have been greater and different results would have occurred.

This argument is consistent with evaluations of the Massachusetts deinstitutionalization experience. An early evaluation found greater recidivism among youths committed to the Department of Youth Services following the closing of the state's training schools, a result similar to that of juveniles released from institutions prior to the reform movement.[53] However, more positive results were found in regions with stronger community-based program implementation. In addition, a later study of the Massachusetts approach found recidivism rates that were as low as or lower than those of most other jurisdictions and were also lower than those of the pre-deinstitutionalization time period.[54]

To continue with the theme of the effects of varying degrees of punishment, several studies have examined the juvenile court's response to offenders referred for the first time. In a series of articles, Brown and colleagues reported on a random sample of 500 juveniles who were adjudicated delinquent in Pennsylvania between 1960 and 1975.[55] Their analyses indicated that while the type of disposition (that is, probation vs. placement facility) was not related to future criminal behavior, adjudication at first court referral was associated with less recidivism than was postponed adjudication. Additionally, juveniles who were not adjudicated on their first referral were two times more likely to end up in prison as adults than were youths who were adjudicated on their first referral.

In a similar study, Jacobs reported slightly different findings. Among first-time juvenile court referrals, youths who were formally processed were less likely to exhibit recidivism than those who were diverted.[56] However, for those juveniles placed under formal court supervision, youths who received out-of-home placements had higher rates of recidivism than did those who received in-home supervision.

Finally, in a similar and more recent study, Minor, Hartmann, and Terry found that there was minimal relationship between type of court action and recidivism for first-time juvenile court referrals.[57] The one exception was that, for people entering adulthood during the follow-up period, those who had been formally petitioned for further processing during the first court action were significantly more likely to be charged in adult court than those who were diverted. Based on these results, the authors concluded that "rather than encouraging high levels of recidivism, extensive and repeated use of diversion in this court was associated with reasonably constrained levels. These findings ... imply that a policy of 'getting tough' with juvenile offenders by petitioning increasingly high proportions of cases, transferring more cases to adult court, and so forth may be misguided."[58]

Deterring Known Youthful Offenders

The findings of Brown and associates, Jacobs, and Minor and colleagues, although varying somewhat, appear consistent with those of Klein, Wooldredge, and Schneider and Ervin. None of these studies found support for the harshest of formal sanctions. Although some of the findings indicate better results from outright release relative to more intermediate community-based programs, the weight of the evidence appears to support formal supervision in a structured community setting. In any event, the results of these studies contrast with those of Murray and Cox and, to a lesser extent, Gottfredson and Barton, who found support for institutionalization rather than other less-restrictive programs. It is important to point out, however, that their research focused on more-serious and frequent offenders. It is possible that the specific deterrent effect of legal punishments varies with the extent of past involvement in delinquent or criminal activity among those who are sanctioned.[59] In other words, formal sanctions might have a different effect on minor offenders than on experienced offenders.

Smith and Gartin found arrest to be associated with an increased probability of lessened criminal activity among less-experienced offenders but not among those in later stages of involvement in criminal activity. Among more-experienced offenders, however, arrest did reduce future rates of offending. Along these same lines, the literature appears to indicate that youths referred to juvenile court for the first time and offenders referred for relatively minor delinquent behavior exhibit less recidivism when they are not forced to undergo incarceration.[60] On the other hand, for the most serious and frequent offenders, institutional confinement might be an effective response that reduces the likelihood of recidivism.[61]

Unfortunately, the final answer is probably not as clear-cut as the previous paragraph would indicate. The findings of Murray and Cox and Gottfredson and Barton are directly contradicted by those of Schneider and Ervin, who also employed a sample of serious and chronic youthful offenders. Furthermore, several longitudinal studies conducted in very diverse locations (London, Philadelphia, and Racine, Wisconsin), suggest that more-severe legal punishments, such as incarceration, lead to increases in future juvenile offending.[62] With these findings in mind, Smith and Gartin concluded:

> The important distinction is that [our] study compares the future criminal activity of those who are offending and punished (arrested) with that of those who are offending but not punished (released by police without arrest). In contrast, the typical study of specific deterrence compares the future criminal activity of two or more groups that differ, not in terms of whether they are punished or not, but in terms of how severely they are punished. It is possible that punishment will reduce future offending relative to no punishment at all, but that among those who are punished, more severe punishment may lead to increased future criminal activity.[63]

JUVENILE TRANSFER AND DETERRENCE

While the studies reviewed to this point examined the general and specific deterrent effects of formal sanctions as applied to a variety of potential and known offenders, a much smaller amount of research has focused on the general and specific deterrent effects of transferring juveniles to adult court. It commonly is assumed by policymakers and the public at large that treating juveniles as adults will reduce overall juvenile crime (that is, have a general deterrent effect) and also reduce or eliminate the future offending of those transferred to criminal court (that is, have a specific deterrent effect). This expectation of greater deterrence is based on the perception that juvenile courts are too lenient and that criminal courts can provide increased accountability and stronger punishment, which will reduce youthful offending. Unfortunately, the anticipated deterrent effects of juvenile transfer often have not been uncovered by research.

General Deterrence from Juvenile Transfer

In terms of general deterrence, four studies have looked at the impact of expanded juvenile transfer laws on aggregate adolescent crime rates. To begin, Singer and McDowall evaluated the effect of New York's legislative waiver law that became effective in 1978.[64] The law lowered the eligible age of criminal justice handling of juveniles to 13 for murder and 14 for other violent offenses. Using Philadelphia data for comparison purposes, the authors conducted a trend analysis of monthly juvenile violent crime arrest rates during the period of 1974 to 1984. The results showed that the law had little measurable effect on juvenile crime and thus did not produce the deterrent effect expected by policymakers.

Similar findings were obtained by Jensen and Metsger, who also used a time series design to assess Idaho's 1981 legislative waiver law that required violent juvenile offenders from ages 14 to 18 to be sent to adult court.[65] Using Montana and Wyoming as comparison states, where similar transfer procedures as those originally existing in Idaho were being employed, yearly juvenile violent crime arrest rates were examined during the periods of 1976 to 1980 and 1982 to 1986. The analysis revealed that violent juvenile crime increased significantly in Idaho following the enactment of the law but decreased in the comparison states, suggesting that the new law had no deterrent effect.

Risler, Sweatman, and Nackerud subsequently assessed the general deterrent effect of Georgia's 1994 legislative waiver law.[66] Juvenile arrest rates were again compared before and after implementation of the new law. The analysis of the 1992–1995 data indicated that there were no significant reductions in arrest rates for the specified waiver offenses, suggesting that the law did not reduce serious juvenile crime.

In contrast to the three studies of the impact of individual state waiver laws discussed above, a recent multistate analysis by Steven Levitt uncovered significant decreases in juvenile crime when states lowered the age at which adult courts assume jurisdiction.[67] Furthermore, declines in crime rates were associated with the transition from juvenile to adult court. Based on data from 1978 to 1993, states that punished people in the first year of their attaining adulthood more harshly relative to juveniles saw violent crime fall by almost 25% and property crime by 15% relative to states in which adult punishments were more lenient. Overall, then, this study found evidence suggesting at least a moderate general deterrent effect from transfer to adult court.

It is difficult to reconcile the findings of Levitt with those of previous researchers, but the safest conclusion appears to be that, at best, expanded waiver laws provide a modest general deterrent effect, but this effect may be small or even nonexistent. Although there is evidence that some juvenile offenders cease or reduce their offending once they reach the official age of adulthood, prior to this time many youths may not be aware of existing or expanded transfer laws and the associated possibility of being prosecuted in adult court.[68] Because other research indicates that the certainty of punishment is more important than severity in producing a general deterrent effect, future research should consider whether stronger implementation and publicizing of transfer laws corresponds with greater deterrence. However, even if expanded waiver laws do have some general deterrent effect, policymakers should recognize that this benefit might be outweighed by the negative effects revealed in research that has examined the future behavior of transferred youths.

Specific Deterrence from Juvenile Transfer

Four other studies have assessed the specific deterrent effect of transferring juveniles to adult court. First, Jeffrey Fagan's previously mentioned research on New York and New Jersey youthful offenders revealed that robbery defendants processed in New York criminal courts were rearrested and reincarcerated at a higher rate than comparable youths in New Jersey juvenile courts, and the New York offenders also were rearrested in a shorter amount of time.[69] In contrast, there were no significant differences for burglary offenders in terms of rearrest, reincarceration, and time until rearrest in juvenile versus adult criminal court.

Second, in their study of matched youths in Florida, Donna Bishop and colleagues found that 30% of the juveniles transferred to adult court were rearrested during a one-year follow-up period, while only 19% of the youths retained in juvenile court were rearrested.[70] Moreover, the mean time to failure was shorter for waived juveniles (135 days) than for retained youths (227 days). Last, there was evidence that recidivism was more serious among youths treated as adults, as 93% of the transferred juveniles who were rearrested were charged with a felony, while 85% of the retained youths who were rearrested were charged with a felony.

In a follow up to this study, the same authors sought to determine whether the short-term differences in recidivism between transferred and retained youths persisted over time for all types of offenders.[71] Approximately six additional years of tracking was conducted to see how the transfer decision affected recidivism over the long term. The analysis showed that youths retained in juvenile court eventually caught up with those transferred to adult court in terms of the prevalence of rearrest, but this was due to an increased probability of rearrest during the long term for retained youths processed on felony property offenses. Once the effect of offense type was controlled, the multivariate analysis indicated that transfer led to more recidivism. Finally, even though transferred property felons were less likely to reoffend, when they did so, they reoffended more frequently and more quickly than did the comparable retained youths.

Third, in their study of juveniles considered for waiver in Hennepin County, Minnesota, Podkopacz and Feld also failed to find evidence of greater specific deterrence in adult criminal court.[72] During a two-year follow-up period, 58% of the transferred offenders were convicted of a new crime in contrast to only 42% of the retained youths. The authors offered three possible explanations for the lower juvenile court recidivism rate: (1) through an emphasis on prior offending, the juvenile court succeeded in transferring the most serious and frequent offenders who had a greater probability of recidivism; (2) treatment services were more effective in the juvenile correctional system; or (3) the adult criminal system better trained (rather than deterred) further criminality than did the juvenile system.

The second and third explanations presented above by Podkopacz and Feld both suggest greater effectiveness in the juvenile court system with regard to handling serious youthful offenders. The first explanation points to the problem of selection bias in this type of research, which would cause greater recidivism to be found among transferred juveniles simply because they are more serious and persistent offenders. However, it is important to consider the fact that none of these explanations would favor a dramatic increase in the number of juveniles who are sent to adult criminal court.

Finally, my research on 557 violent youthful offenders processed in Pennsylvania juvenile and adult courts in 1994 also found evidence of greater recidivism among transferred youths during both the predispositional and postdispositional stages of processing.[73] Of the 224 offenders who were released from predispositional secure custody, those in adult court were more likely to be rearrested and also exhibited more serious predispositional recidivism compared with their counterparts in juvenile court. Similarly, during an 18-month post-dispositional follow-up period, the transferred youths displayed greater, more serious, and faster recidivism than did offenders retained in juvenile court, while controlling for a variety of offense and offender characteristics. In sum, these findings support those of previous studies that found no evidence of a specific deterrent effect from juvenile transfer to adult criminal court.

SUMMARY AND CONCLUSIONS

During the past 30 years, there has been increasing public and political support for various get tough on crime strategies. The most popular approaches have been those that promise the harshest punishment. While often supported on the grounds of increased retribution and incapacitation, a central argument of this movement has been that stronger punishments are needed to deter crime. Treating juvenile offenders as adults fits in well with this view, as the criminal court is expected to provide formal sanctions that are greater and more effective than those imposed in juvenile court. In turn, this response to youthful offending is expected to have a beneficial impact on juvenile crime.

Juvenile transfer is an extreme response to youthful offending with potentially severe consequences. As discussed in previous chapters, youths who are treated as adults often are subjected to a lengthy adjudicatory process, sometimes involving an extended stay in jail, a criminal conviction, and a prolonged prison sentence. With regard to the conditions of confinement, juveniles in adult jails and prisons appear to receive less-adequate treatment services and are more likely to be violently victimized than similar offenders in juvenile correctional facilities. Subjecting juveniles to this potentially harsh punishment essentially is viewed as being necessary for enhanced public safety.

At question, however, is whether any increase in punishment severity obtained through juvenile transfer provides beneficial consequences. While a major justification for waiver to adult court is the deterrence of juvenile crime, the studies that have addressed this issue have failed to establish the expected general and specific deterrent effects. Although several studies on general deterrence and Levitt's research on juvenile crime and punishment do provide some evidence of a general deterrent effect from formal sanctions, three other studies did not find this effect from expanded waiver laws. Furthermore, as Bishop and colleagues noted in their study of Florida youths, short-term gains achieved through harsher sanctioning can be offset by greater recidivism once offenders are released from confinement.

Based on the research discussed in this chapter, it would appear that legal punishments can have a specific deterrent effect but that increasingly harsher sanctions might have little additional impact and could actually lead to greater recidivism. This conclusion would seem to support the specific deterrent effect of certain punishments rather than more severe punishments, which contrasts with the basic philosophy of the get tough movement. However, the final answer to the question of whether formal sanctions, including those resulting from transfer, produce a specific deterrent effect might be closer to the argument of Lawrence Sherman, who proposed that legal punishments can either reduce, increase, or have no effect on future criminal activity depending on a variety of factors related to the offender, offense, and social setting.[74]

In presenting a theory of "defiance," Sherman argued that the future criminal behavior of formally sanctioned individuals will be influenced by such things as the degree to which offenders perceive the sanctioning as legitimate, the strength of social bonds that offenders have with the sanctioning agent and community, and the extent to which offenders accept the sanctioning without becoming angry and feeling rejected.

Research has shown that individuals tend to obey the law more when they believe a criminal sanction has been administered fairly.[75] Furthermore, randomized experiments in arrest for domestic violence have found arrest to reduce repeat domestic violence among employed men but increase it among those who are unemployed.[76] More importantly, there is at least limited evidence that older people, who generally have more of a stake in conformity, are more effectively deterred by formal sanctions than are younger people.[77]

If juveniles are less likely than adults to be deterred by formal sanctions, it also may be a result of the legitimacy they perceive in legal punishments. It is well known that virtually all youths commit some type of delinquent act, yet many or most are not caught or formally sanctioned.[78] In discussing their findings of a criminogenic effect of punishment on future delinquent behavior, Paternoster and Piquero asserted:

> In understanding the point that imposed sanctions may backfire, and lead to additional offending, it should be kept in mind that most of the offenders in this sample offended without consequence. It is entirely possible that those youths who committed delinquent acts and did get caught and sanctioned saw their punishment as unfair. When so many others "get away with it," their own apprehension for offending may have been a bitter enough experience for the infrequently punished to become defiant.[79]

Overall, available scientific research does not support the idea that juvenile transfer to adult court can provide much in the way of general or specific deterrent effects on juvenile crime. When combined with the evidence and information presented in previous chapters, a more limited use of waiver is warranted rather than the expanded provisions adopted in most states during the past two decades.

CHAPTER 8

The Rise and Fall of "Adult Crime, Adult Time"

During the 1990s, both the American public and policymakers voiced strong support for transferring greater numbers and types of serious and violent juvenile offenders to adult criminal court. Public opinion polls from this decade found that roughly three quarters of surveyed citizens favored the use of this policy. However, some of this research also indicated that many of those questioned did not support giving juveniles the same sentences as adults or placing these youths in adult correctional facilities, and there was less public backing for waiving younger, as opposed to older, adolescents. Finally, perceptions that other sentencing and correctional alternatives were ineffective seemed to be an important factor in shaping public opinion. Policymakers appeared to agree with some, but not all, of these beliefs, resulting in virtually all states passing legislation to facilitate the transfer of juveniles to adult court.

Most of the information and evidence presented in previous chapters shows that an overreliance on juvenile transfer to control and reduce youthful offending is a misguided approach. Following nearly two centuries of efforts to distinguish juvenile offenders from adult criminals, there is little reason to believe that policies seeking to prosecute larger numbers of youths as adults will produce much in the way of desirable consequences. Older, male, nonwhite, and poor juveniles from urban areas continue to represent the majority of waived adolescents. Research further suggests that discretion built into many modern transfer laws has resulted in similar, rather than larger, numbers and types of offenders actually being prosecuted, convicted, and sentenced in adult court. Moreover, while studies of case outcomes for youths in adult court do not consistently reveal findings that correspond with public and political expectations, older and more-violent juvenile offenders appear to be the ones actually punished harshly in the adult criminal system.

Contemporary studies also have shown that a variety of programs can effectively rehabilitate serious and violent youthful offenders, particularly in the juvenile system, and that juvenile correctional facilities are better prepared to safely house and treat these young people. In addition, the evidence indicates that we can expect a marginal general-deterrent effect, at best, from expanded use or threat of use of waiver to adult court, but this possible beneficial effect likely is offset by greater and more serious future offending among transferred youths (rather than lesser offending as a result of specific deterrence). In sum, what is known about the effectiveness of transferring juveniles to adult court indicates that a more selective approach to this practice is warranted rather than trying to waive increasingly younger and broader categories of youthful offenders.

Other current issues pertaining to juvenile transfer to adult court and the future of juvenile transfer policies and practices must still be considered. Recent trends in youth violence, along with emerging evidence regarding adolescent development and offending contribute to the ongoing debate regarding juvenile transfer, and the issue of capital punishment for juveniles is one of continuing concern and discussion. Considering what the future of juvenile transfer holds must be based on sound knowledge and scientific evidence rather than unfounded assumptions and politically charged motives.

RECENT TRENDS IN YOUTH VIOLENCE

We have learned that from the mid-1980s until the mid-1990s, America experienced a surge in recorded incidences of youth violence.[1] This was accompanied by relatively stable trends in serious juvenile property offending. Since 1994, though, juvenile arrest rates for both violent crime and serious property crime have declined steadily.[2] In fact, juvenile arrest rates for serious and violent crimes are at a 20-year low, and youth violence no longer is at the top of the list of public and political concerns.

Instead, fears about terrorism and an emphasis on homeland security have taken center stage.

There are current signs that trends and patterns in juvenile offending might soon change. Many have noted that with diminished public and financial support for prevention and intervention programs, declines in violent youthful offending have diminished, and increases again are being observed. For example, in Boston, a city well-known for its dramatic decreases in youth violence during the latter half of the 1990s, the number of young murder victims younger than 24 has nearly doubled during a one-year period.[3] This follows several years of federal and state funding cuts. In 2001, the Boston Housing Authority lost $3.1 million in federal funds that supported youth services, eventually resulting in the closure of youth centers in 15 housing developments.[4] State Department of Public Health funding that supported 10 outreach workers at various Boston nonprofit agencies also was cut, along with state support for youth summer jobs. This situation has led Emmett Folgert, a longtime director of the Dorchester Youth Collaborative, to conclude, "Let's be clear: There is no 'Boston Strategy' without a certain level of funding. That level of funding doesn't exist right now."[5]

Nationally, gang violence also has reemerged as a disturbing issue.[6] Annual gang-related homicides across the country declined from more than 1,200 in 1995 to fewer than 700 in 1999 but since then have risen to more than 1,000 in 2003. More than 40% of the 2,182 cities responding to the 2002 National Gang Survey reported that gang activity was "getting worse" (an increase from 27% the previous year), and 87% of U.S. cities with populations of at least 100,000 reported problems with gangs. In Denver, Colorado, budget cuts forced the elimination of the district attorney's antigang unit in 2002 before it was reestablished in 2003. While commenting on these developments, Tim Twining, director of gang prosecutions in Denver, stated, "We had a chance to pull the weeds out of our communities for good a few years ago.... We didn't do it. We got distracted. Now the weeds are back."[7]

These signs of reversing trends in youth violence and gang activity come not only at a time when attention and resources have been shifted elsewhere but also when the U.S. juvenile population is projected to grow well into the foreseeable future.[8] More juveniles combined with rising rates of youth violence and a lack of adequate funding and resources is a recipe for disaster. Furthermore, if recent trends continue, it is quite likely that by the time a growing problem with serious and violent youthful offending is recognized, policymakers will react by supporting another crackdown effort that again encourages greater use of juvenile transfer to adult court. The information and evidence contained in these pages suggest that this is the wrong approach upon which to rely, and greater use of knowledge about adolescent development and the effectiveness of prevention and early intervention programs and strategies is needed.

ADOLESCENT DEVELOPMENT

At their root level, juvenile transfer policies assume that adolescents will rationally consider the consequences of their actions, will know about and understand the provisions provided in transfer laws, and therefore will choose not to commit serious and violent crime (that is, they will experience general deterrence). Furthermore, if they do decide to commit these illegal acts, the experience of being waived to adult court and subsequently punished will cause them to choose law-abiding behavior upon their return to society (that is, they will experience specific deterrence). The information and evidence presented in Chapter 7 questions these assumptions on the basis that it is likely that adolescents typically do not think about and weigh the consequences of their behavior in the same manner as adults.

The teenagers commonly targeted by juvenile transfer laws often are psychosocially immature and have experienced a variety of negative life circumstances or risk factors, contributing to their impulsive behavior, limited perspective on life, and propensity for engaging in risk-taking to achieve short-term gains while disregarding long-term consequences.[9] This statement seems particularly true for younger adolescents (such as in the Nathaniel Abraham case), although "there would appear to be a scientific basis within the psychological literature on adolescent development for distinguishing under the law between individuals who have, versus have not, reached the age of 17."[10] In other words, the lack of maturity of judgment displayed in early through mid-adolescence seems to make the rational assumption of deterrence theory less applicable to juveniles.[11]

In addition, interviews with justice system officials reveal that young offenders often do not know about or comprehend juvenile transfer laws and that these youths tend to place more emphasis on the rewards to be gained from illegal acts than on the potential punishments.[12] These rewards can include money or material possessions, but status is perhaps a more commonly desired outcome. As reported by a juvenile court judge from a large metropolitan area in Pennsylvania:

> Kids don't think about what they do. They don't question the penalty. Some don't even know the penalty, and most don't care.... Deterrence only works for people with something to lose. These kids will never be wearing a paisley tie and talking to someone about their Ph.D. The only thing that's important is having respect among their friends, and the law isn't going to make any difference to them.... Status is gained in the inner city by being a dominant male. They need to use a gun because respect in the neighborhood is the most important thing. You can't be a pussy.... We need to tell the truth about this: You can't deter someone from something they have to do.[13]

In sum, the belief in the deterrent value of juvenile transfer laws appears unfounded, and it is more likely that waiving youths to adult court sets the stage for inferior treatment, violent victimization, learning from adult criminals, and negative labeling effects to occur. When these youths are returned to the community, as most are within a few years of their criminal processing, they generally face limited job prospects, the effects of stigmatization and victimization, poor living conditions, and possibly a perceived sense of injustice and unfair treatment. Yet we expect that broad, reactionary transfer policies and practices will provide a beneficial impact on juvenile crime. Fortunately, there is an alternative path available, which has begun to be employed but currently is being threatened by funding and program priority shifts.

PREVENTION AND INTERVENTION EFFECTIVENESS

Since the early 1990s, there has been growing support for a more comprehensive, collaborative, and integrative approach to dealing with serious and violent juvenile offending.[14] This strategy is based on research regarding the causes and correlates of delinquency, effective prevention and early intervention efforts, and successful treatment and rehabilitation programs. Rather than responding to youth violence after it has escalated to a high level, as juvenile transfer to adult court seeks to do, the evidence suggests that a combination of prevention and early intervention programs with a coordinated system of treatment and graduated sanctions will be more effective in reducing juvenile crime. This is reflective of the use of a public health model for dealing with crime and delinquency as opposed to the reactive war on crime and get tough movements that are characterized by their emphasis on retribution, incapacitation, and deterrence.

Using the public health approach, risk factors that predict future adolescent and adult problem behaviors are identified and targeted for prevention and intervention purposes, with the belief that reducing risk factors will lower future crime and delinquency. These risk factors can exist within communities (for example, availability of alcohol and drugs, norms favorable to drug use and crime, poverty, and physical deterioration), families (for example, family conflict and management problems, favorable parental attitudes and involvement in problem behaviors, and child abuse and neglect), schools (for example, academic failure, low commitment to school), and individuals (for example, cognitive deficits, early onset of problem behaviors, delinquent or criminal peers, and favorable attitudes toward problem behaviors). In addition to assessing and reducing risk, efforts also are directed at increasing protective factors associated with healthy childhood and adolescent development. These include strong parental bonds with children starting at an early age, providing opportunities and recognition for positive behavior, improving parenting skills and childhood learning skills, and establishing and maintaining healthy community beliefs and clear standards for behavior.[15]

This approach has been supported at the national level by the Office of Juvenile Justice and Delinquency Prevention (OJJDP). From 1994 to 2002, OJJDP provided more than $1 billion in funding through its Community Prevention Grants Program to aid states and communities with the implementation of strategies to reduce risk factors, enhance protective factors, and decrease adolescent problem behaviors.[16] These funds have assisted more than 1,200 communities across the country and generally have contributed to more broad-based community representation, better integration of local prevention efforts, and stronger leveraging of resources for long-term sustainability and success.

Another result of this federal movement and funding has been the adoption of Communities That Care (CTC) in more than 400 localities nationwide.[17] CTC is an operating system designed to prevent delinquency, substance abuse, teen pregnancy, school dropout, and violence, with an emphasis on using community-level research to identify priority risk and protective factors and then implement programs that have been shown through research to be effective in reducing risk, enhancing protection, and preventing future crime and delinquency.[18] The Commonwealth of Pennsylvania is an example of a state that has embraced this approach, as approximately 125 communities have adopted CTC through the support of the Governor's Partnership for Safe Children and the Pennsylvania Commission on Crime and Delinquency.[19]

In combination with proactive prevention efforts, a more integrated and coordinated system of intervention, rehabilitation, and sanctioning is necessary to reduce youthful offending. Nearly 10 years ago, in discussing the progression of delinquency toward chronic and violent behavior, Barry Krisberg and colleagues asserted:

> The lack of consistent intervention with juvenile offenders soon after their initial contact with the police or other referring agency has long been recognized as perhaps the single largest gap in services for troubled youth, including serious, violent, and chronic juvenile offenders.... Too often, the juvenile justice system's response early in a young offender's career is either too much or too little.... It gives rise to an all-too-common pattern: repeated encounters with authorities, perhaps coupled with several short-term detentions, but with no coherent or intensive help provided, culminating in repeated offenses and, ultimately, incarceration in the juvenile and adult systems.[20]

A decade later, services to children and families are still being described as fragmented, crisis-oriented, rigid, isolated, insufficiently funded, and mismanaged.[21] Problem children and families often are known to more than one social service agency, but individual agencies commonly are not aware of or fully informed about other agency services being provided. Social service agencies also typically do not work closely with juvenile courts, particularly when dealing with younger children who may just be starting their delinquent and criminal careers. This happens despite the strong relationship that exists between early onset and later chronic delinquency and violent behavior.[22] However, there is evidence that when a comprehensive, community-wide strategy is employed that facilitates not only collaboration among agencies but actual integration of services, these problems can be overcome.

The most prominent advocate of the "comprehensive strategy" has been James C. Howell.[23] Based on a substantial collection of research and supportive scientific findings, Howell has argued strongly that when community-based prevention and early intervention efforts are combined with an integrated system of graduated sanctions and a continuum of treatment alternatives, secure institutions are needed only for the most serious, chronic, and violent offenders. This also would reduce our reliance on transfer to adult court as a major policy option. The use of CTC illustrates the prevention and early intervention component of this strategy. North Carolina serves as an example of a state that has implemented the additional graduated system of sanctioning and treatment recommended by Howell and characterized by offender risk assessment, matching of services with offender needs, and integrating programs that have been found effective in reducing risk factors and future offending.[24]

The development of comprehensive prevention, intervention, sanctioning, and treatment strategies corresponded in time with declining rates of serious and violent juvenile offending. Recent shifts in funding and other resources, though, have coincided with signs that stable juvenile crime rates might soon exhibit an upturn at the same time that the juvenile population continues to increase. It is therefore important to stress that contemporary investments in children and youths should not be lost because of a renewed faith in punishment-oriented practices (such as transfer to adult court) that are politically wise but limited in their benefits to society.

JUVENILE COURT ABOLITION AND REFORM

Despite encouraging evidence from studies of modern juvenile treatment and rehabilitation programs and less-than-supportive scientific findings concerning the effectiveness of transferring larger numbers of offenders to adult criminal court, there are those who believe that the juvenile court should be abolished or at least reconceptualized in a way that greatly removes illegal behavior from its jurisdiction. Barry Feld most notably stands out as a proponent for juvenile court abolition,[25] while Mark Moore and Stewart Wakeling are representative of the reconceptualization movement.[26]

Feld's support for abolition is based on his belief that juvenile courts have become more punitive and less, rather than more, effective over time in treating and rehabilitating youths; that juvenile courts fail to provide adequate due process rights; and that all offenders would be better served in one integrated criminal court. He further asserts that current knowledge about adolescent development could be used to formulate a "youth discount" that would allow shorter sentences to be imposed on younger offenders; incarcerated adolescents could be housed in age-segregated correctional facilities; and one integrated system would provide better record keeping, legal representation, and procedural justice. Overall, this system would "provide young offenders with greater protections and justice than they currently receive in the juvenile system, and more proportional and humane consequences than judges presently inflict on them in the criminal justice system."[27]

At first glance, Feld's arguments appear to have some merit, but then one is reminded of the old adage, "If it sounds too good to be true, it probably is." Inadequate treatment and rehabilitation services, poor legal representation, and due process violations certainly do occur in the juvenile justice system. However, available evidence indicates the adult criminal system is ill-prepared to process, sanction, and rehabilitate an influx of preadolescent and teenage offenders and that the juvenile system actually does a commendable job of doing so, particularly when huge differences in funding and resources between the two systems are considered. Moreover, the case of SCI Pine Grove serves to illustrate what happens when good intentions meet reality: A costly state prison designed specifically for transferred youths now stands filled mostly with adult criminal inmates because plans for an age-segregated facility were changed in an effort to address problems with overcrowding in other state prisons. Abolishing the juvenile court is, at best, a risky proposition that would require an extremely difficult and expensive reorganization effort to succeed but also would present a greater potential for causing more harm than good.

Rather than arguing that juvenile courts should be abolished, Moore and Wakeling contend that they should be reconceptualized as courts for "bankrupt families."[28] These authors note that critics of American juvenile justice have come from both ends of the political spectrum, as those from the Left have focused on the intrusiveness, unfairness, and ineffectiveness of juvenile courts and those from the Right have concentrated on a perceived failure of juvenile courts to hold offenders accountable and protect society. To address this situation, Moore and Wakeling propose that rather than pursuing a criminalization movement in juvenile justice, more of a family court model should be employed that oversees families who are failing to meet their obligations to children and society. Within this model, greater emphasis would be placed on society's responsibility to children, relying on social science research to guide the court, and a stronger investment in an array of social services.

Again, at first glance the position of Moore and Wakeling has merit. In fact, much of the evidence examined in this book would support their proposal. The difficulty here, however, is the political and public opposition that would result from including older, more-serious, and more-violent juvenile delinquents in a newly conceptualized family court that would be perceived by many as being too soft to handle anything but families with children and early adolescents who have not yet exhibited much in the way of illegal behavior. A real possibility exists that a family court like this would have limited jurisdiction for younger, predelinquent youths, while teenagers (for example, age 14 and older) who break the law (for example, commit a misdemeanor or felony) would be processed in adult criminal court. This system essentially would look much the same as if the juvenile court simply was abolished as a method of handling delinquent youths, and it would pose the same dangers inherent in the abolition movement.

JUVENILES AND THE DEATH PENALTY

Some proponents of transferring juveniles to adult court believe that this practice provides the additional benefit of allowing these offenders to be subjected to the death penalty. Support for juvenile capital punishment tends to center on many of the same issues presented by advocates of juvenile transfer, including retribution, incapacitation, and deterrence. In other words, from this perspective capital punishment is needed for adolescents in cases where death is an appropriate punishment for the worst crimes, and, as a result, permanent incapacitation will be achieved and general deterrence will be enhanced. The death penalty for juveniles recently has received increased attention and deserves some mention in the context of juvenile waiver, since transfer to adult court must occur for this penalty to be imposed.

In a series of cases heard in the 1980s, the U.S. Supreme Court basically established that individuals committing a capital offense (for example, certain forms of murder) at the age of 16 or older can be executed after being found guilty in criminal court.[29] As of June 2000, 74 adults (ranging in age from 18 to 41 years old) were housed on death row in 16 different states for crimes committed before they turned 18.[30] All were male, about three quarters committed their crimes at age 17, nearly two thirds were minorities, and some have been awaiting execution for more than 20 years. In the past 30 years, fewer than 20 men actually have been put to death for crimes they committed as juveniles, and about half of these were from one state, Texas.

Thirty-eight states and the federal government currently authorize the death penalty, and more than 3,500 prisoners are housed in America with a sentence of death.[31] This means that death row inmates who committed their crimes prior to age 18 represent just 2% of the total death row population. Moreover, only 22 states and the federal government allow capital punishment to be imposed on those who were 16 or 17 at the time of their offense. The use of the death penalty for juveniles in these jurisdictions distinguishes the United States as being among only a small number of countries that continue this practice. This list includes Bangladesh, Iran, Iraq, Nigeria, Pakistan, Saudi Arabia, and Yemen.[32] In recent years, several other countries, such as China, that have historically upheld the death penalty have changed their laws to state that capital punishment will not be imposed for offenses committed by persons younger than 18.

In addition to the fact that the United States is one of only a few countries in the world to impose death on juvenile offenders and that less than half of all American states allow for this practice (and even fewer actually use it), there are other reasons to reject capital punishment as a sanctioning option for juveniles. First, research indicates that the general deterrent effect expected from the death penalty is highly suspect at best, and there is some evidence that executions actually are associated with increases in homicides (that is, a brutalization rather than deterrent effect).[33] Based on what is known about adolescent development and the overall weak evidence of any general deterrent effect from juvenile transfer to adult court, it seems very unlikely that a general deterrent effect is achieved through the possibility of capital punishment being in place for juveniles.

Second, as is the case in the use of juvenile transfer, substantial racial and class disparities exist with regard to imposition and execution of the death penalty. More than half of all death row inmates are African

American or Hispanic,[34] and a number of studies have found that the race of the offender and especially the race of the victim impact on death penalty outcomes.[35] Killers of whites, in particular, are significantly more likely to receive capital punishment than killers of African Americans. Furthermore, overrepresentation of minority group members corresponds with death penalty defendants predominantly coming from the lower class. The fact that southern states (particularly Texas, Florida, North Carolina, Alabama, Georgia, and Oklahoma) are responsible for quite a bit more than half of all death sentences and roughly six out of every seven executions[36] combines with racial and class disparities to suggest that the death penalty simply is applied in an unfair manner.

Third, there has been decreasing public support for the death penalty in general and even less support for applying capital punishment to juveniles. While less than two thirds of polled Americans currently voice some support for the death penalty (down from more than three quarters a decade ago), when the alternative of a life sentence without the possibility of parole is presented, support for the death penalty drops to about 50%.[37] In addition, about half of all nationwide respondents believe that the death penalty is applied unequally to African Americans and whites for the same crime; roughly two thirds believe that poor people are more likely than people with greater income to receive the death penalty and that capital punishment is unfair because of geographical differences in its use; eight of every 10 believe that an innocent person has been executed in the United States; and seven of every 10 favor a moratorium on the death penalty until questions about its fairness can be resolved. Finally, fewer than half of polled Americans support the use of capital punishment for juveniles, and many of those are willing to accept a life sentence without the possibility of parole as an alternative.[38]

In response to some of the facts and figures presented above, in August 2003 the Missouri Supreme Court ruled that the execution of people for crimes they committed before their eighteenth birthday violated the Eighth and Fourteenth Amendments of the U.S. Constitution.[39] In the case of Christopher Simmons,[40] a 17-year-old juvenile convicted of first-degree murder, the Missouri Supreme Court relied heavily on the U.S. Supreme Court's 2002 decision in *Atkins v. Virginia*.[41] In *Atkins*, it was determined that the execution of mentally retarded inmates violated the

U.S. Constitution because a national consensus had emerged against such executions. In deciding *Simmons*, the Missouri Supreme Court specifically considered modern legislative action on the death penalty, frequency of imposition of capital punishment on juveniles, national and international opinion, and its own assessment of whether the death penalty is warranted for juveniles for purposes of deterrence and retribution.

In the end, the Missouri Supreme Court reasoned that the U.S. Supreme Court would hold that the execution of persons for crimes they committed when younger than 18 violates the "evolving standards of decency" in American society, and, consequently, Christopher Simmons was resentenced to life without parole. The foundation for the Missouri court's decision will be tested soon, as the U.S. Supreme Court recently decided to accept *Roper v. Simmons* for further review.[42] The outcome of this case might essentially end future use of the death penalty for juveniles, but, if not, there is little reason to believe that continued use of juvenile capital punishment will provide much benefit to American society.

THE FUTURE OF JUVENILE TRANSFER

Will transferring juveniles to adult court come to an end in the United States? The answer is probably "no." As long as there is a separate system of justice in place for dealing with children and youths, which very likely will continue to be the case in the future, there also will be a perceived need and desire to treat some of these young people as adults. Few would argue that there are not certain older, chronic, and violent adolescent offenders who, for the sake of public safety, should be removed from society for long periods of time. Moreover, waiver to adult court will continue to exist because of its symbolic importance. Society can use this procedure to express both its fear of serious and violent youth crime and its revulsion for the young offenders who commit it. Having this symbolic importance makes juvenile transfer more resistant to rational and scientific arguments. Nonetheless, the information and evidence contained in this book indicates that extending the transfer of juveniles beyond those who are deemed the "most deserving" is not good public policy. The real issue, then, is not whether youthful offenders should be waived to adult court but which juveniles should be transferred and how they should be processed and sanctioned once they get there.

Who Should Be Transferred?

While juvenile court judges are likely to retain the ability to waive at least some youths to adult court (that is, the use of judicial waiver will continue but on a relatively limited basis), the modern use of legislative waiver, lowering the minimum age for adult court jurisdiction, and, to a lesser extent, prosecutorial waiver are apt to continue. However, rather than statutorily excluding broad categories of offenders from juvenile court or encouraging prosecutors to file charges directly in adult court for large numbers of juvenile cases, the available evidence points to a more selective approach. Youths who are charged with murder undoubtedly will continue to be targeted for legislative or prosecutorial waiver. Still, the possibility of decertification or reverse waiver should exist for these adolescents, and a minimum age of at least 14 for a murder defendant to be criminally prosecuted seems appropriate. Furthermore, the placement of other serious and violent youthful offenders in adult court should be reduced in scope and practice.

To begin, various sources suggest that 75% or more of all transferred youths are 16 or older.[43] As revealed in Chapter 4, not only is offense at an older age associated with a greater likelihood of transfer, but preliminary studies on decertification indicate younger adolescents are more likely to receive reverse waiver than are their older counterparts. These findings, in combination with what is known about adolescent development and decision-making, suggest that a minimum age of 16 should be the standard for adult court processing and prison intervention, at least for all crimes other than murder. This would ensure that younger adolescents could receive juvenile correctional services and also avoid the potential negative consequences of contact with adult criminals and public labeling in the adult system.

Next, instead of using broad categories of serious and violent offenses for transfer eligibility, a focus on firearms seems more justified. Firearm use was a key factor in the surge in youth violence that took place from the mid-1980s to the mid-1990s,[44] particularly with regard to the rapid increases that occurred in the juvenile murder arrest rate and juvenile murder victimization rate.[45] Research also shows that violent juvenile gun users receive the most immediate attention and severe sanctions in adult court and that justice system officials believe waiver laws should target gun offenses.[46]

In general, from a public safety standpoint, focusing transfer laws on juvenile firearm users would offer the best chance of providing both immediate and longer-term protection. However, not all adolescent gun users are equal in terms of their behaviors and future risk to society, and there is some evidence that transferred firearm users exhibit greater recidivism than do firearm users who are retained in juvenile court.[47] These findings imply that transferred gun users are the most chronic violent offenders and that juvenile courts can deal effectively with at least some youths who resort to firearm violence. Therefore, identifying some other factor or factors to consider in combination with firearm use may be appropriate in determining which offenders require longer-term periods of incapacitation in the adult system.

Not surprisingly, a youth's prior offending history may supply the needed information. Offenders with more serious and extensive offending backgrounds tend to be given more immediate attention and are punished more severely, particularly in adult court, but these same youths also exhibit a greater risk for recidivism.[48] This implies that adolescents with substantial histories of offending are more likely to continue their chronic behavior into young adulthood, despite the imposition of harsher punishment.

Based on the combined research findings concerning firearm use and prior offending history, it seems logical to suggest that waiver laws target both of these factors together. In other words, older youths who both employ a gun and display a notable delinquent background should be the focus of juvenile transfer. While use of a firearm during the commission of a violent act would appear fairly easy to define, specifying the needed prior record could prove more difficult. One option would be to require a prior adjudication of delinquency on a violent felony offense. Another would be to develop a prior-record scoring system, common in adult sentencing guidelines, that could take into account all prior adjudications. In any event, if a youth's offending history is going to take a more prominent role in the transfer process and adult court sanctioning, juvenile records must be improved and made more accessible, at least for those working in the juvenile and criminal justice systems.[49]

Sanctioning Serious and Violent Juvenile Offenders

If the above recommendations were followed, juveniles in the adult criminal justice system would be older and more-violent adolescents who pose the greatest threat to public safety. This would reduce the likelihood of negative experiences and longer-term adverse consequences for younger and less-serious offenders and would allow for lengthy incapacitation of the most dangerous youths. This approach contrasts with most modern waiver laws that encompass broad categories of younger, less-serious, and lower-risk juveniles,[50] and it also would require greater consideration of how serious and violent young offenders will be processed and sanctioned in both the juvenile and adult systems.

One justification posed for transferring older youths is that these offenders are about to reach the age of criminal court jurisdiction, so juvenile courts should allow adult courts to handle their cases. This practice of transferring older juveniles, even if they lack a violent offense or substantial offending history, is unquestionably influenced by a perceived need for longer sentences than are available in the juvenile system, and previous arguments have been made that waiver should occur only when an appropriate term of confinement greatly exceeds the period available in juvenile court.[51] Many may feel, though, that even very young violent offenders should be transferred because of the finite ability of juvenile courts to maintain custody and supervision. However, other options exist and should be further explored and studied.

Although there are exceptions, most states use 18 as the age at which criminal courts receive jurisdiction over young offenders.[52] However, almost all states also define a maximum age greater than 18 for which the juvenile court can retain custody and supervision beyond the original age of jurisdiction. Juvenile courts in most states can retain control to age 21, but in a few (California, Montana, Oregon, and Wisconsin), the juvenile court can retain jurisdiction for certain offenses to age 25. Offenders in these states cannot be tried again for the same offense after reaching age 18, but the juvenile court can maintain supervision or custody.

Rather than waiving increased numbers of juveniles, both young and old, to adult court, an alternative in most states would be to raise the maximum age at which the juvenile court can retain jurisdiction (that is, to age 24 or 25). This option would allow for lengthier confinement and supervision when needed and would avoid many of the adverse consequences and negative outcomes associated with sending youths to adult court. Furthermore, raising the maximum age at which juvenile courts can maintain jurisdiction would be in accordance with the fact that crime, including violent offending, peaks by late adolescence and declines thereafter.[53] It only seems logical, then, that juvenile courts should be able to keep control of known offenders into young adulthood rather than "cutting them loose" at a time when they are most likely to break the law. To fully implement this approach, however, would require a greater investment in youths and the juvenile justice system and likely a shift in some funding and resources currently devoted to dealing with young adult offenders in the criminal justice system.

Another alternative is greater, but more consistent, use of the blended jurisdiction or blended sentencing schemes discussed in Chapter 3. In general, this approach seeks to achieve proportionality and heighten formal control by combining juvenile and adult sanctions. In sentencing youthful offenders, some states allow adult criminal courts to impose a sanction involving either juvenile or adult correctional services (or both, in some states). Other states have enabled juvenile courts to identify certain offenders for special processing and sanctioning, which may or may not include relocation to adult correctional facilities at some future point.

If a goal is to avoid the potential negative consequences that arise from transfer to adult court, blended sentencing options that retain most youths in juvenile court appear to have the most potential for effectiveness. Fifteen states currently employ versions of juvenile blended sentencing laws.[54] Although slightly different in various ways, these laws and their associated practices generally focus on serious and violent youthful offenders who have not been waived to adult court. While the right to move certain cases to the adult system at a later date is preserved, the overriding purpose of this approach is to maintain access to juvenile correctional services and provide longer periods of supervision, control, and custody under the jurisdiction of the juvenile court.

Even if extended juvenile court jurisdiction and juvenile blended sentencing options are pursued and strengthened, there will still be a relatively small group of older, chronic, and more-violent adolescent offenders who will be prosecuted in adult court and will likely end up in adult jails and prisons. Minimally, they should be segregated from the rest of the adult inmate population, preferably until the age at which juvenile court jurisdiction would end if these offenders were retained in the juvenile system (for example, at least age 21 but perhaps age 24 or 25). A better approach would be to provide smaller and separate adult correctional facilities and treatment services for these youths, since many will be returned to society and will be expected to be productive and law-abiding community members upon their release.

The main advantage that adult correctional facilities hold for the most-deserving offenders is the length of incarceration and treatment that can be provided. Beyond the benefit of greater incapacitation that lengthier imprisonment can provide, some research suggests that for the most-serious, chronic, and violent youthful offenders, longer-term institutional confinement can reduce the likelihood of recidivism.[55] This may be the result of deterrence, rehabilitation, maturation, or some combination of effects from longer periods of incarceration, but the evidence reviewed in Chapter 6 suggests that contemporary treatment and rehabilitation efforts can be effective, even with the worst juvenile offenders. However, risk and needs assessments, program development and matching, and researcher involvement in program implementation and evaluation (all associated with program effectiveness) are not quick, easy, and cheap, so once again, a greater public investment in youths exhibiting serious and violent behaviors is necessary for this approach to succeed.

FINAL CONCLUSIONS

The key lesson to be learned from more than 100 years of experience with transferring juveniles to adult court is that this practice is not a panacea for serious and violent juvenile offending. The threat and use of harsher adult court sanctions, and even the death penalty (if it is not abolished for juveniles), will not provide substantial general and specific deterrent effects for young offenders. As long as we continue our reactive approach to adolescent problem behavior, cycles of serious and violent youth crime will be met with calls for greater use of juvenile transfer. As informed citizens, though, we could take on the responsibilities of influencing public officials and making a greater investment in children and youths through a more proactive approach to preventing and reducing delinquency and youth violence. We are beginning to more fully understand childhood and adolescent development as well as what works to guide children toward success in life and correct adolescent problem behavior. What we choose to do with this information will go a long way in determining how future generations of young people are viewed.

Notes

Chapter 1 "Adult Crime, Adult Time"

1. Cable News Network, 1999, 2000; Moore, 2000.

2. Merlo & Benekos, 2000.

3. Transfer and waiver are the two most commonly used terms to represent the process of placing a juvenile offender in adult court for prosecution. Certification and remand are used less frequently. Throughout this book, these words will be used interchangeably.

4. Sickmund, Snyder, & Poe-Yamagata, 1997; Torbet et al., 1996; Torbet & Szymanski, 1998.

5. Greenwood, 1995.

6. Farrington, Ohlin, & Wilson, 1986, p. 125.

7. Howell, 1996, p. 50.

8. Cook & Laub, 1998; Snyder & Sickmund, 1999.

9. Snyder & Sickmund, 1999, p. 120.

10. Sickmund et al., 1997, p. 18.

11. Cook & Laub, 1998; Fagan & Wilkinson, 1998; Zimring, 1998.

12. Snyder & Sickmund, 1999, p. 126.

13. Moore & Tonry, 1998, pp. 8–16.

14. Blumstein, 1995; Blumstein, Cohen, Roth, & Visher, 1986; Farrington, 1986, 1998.

15. Farrington, 1998; Howell, 1997, 2003; Howell, Krisberg, Hawkins, & Wilson, 1995; Loeber & Farrington, 1999.

16. E. Anderson, 1998.

17. Howell, 2003; Howell & Hawkins, 1998; Loeber & Farrington, 1999.

18. Moore & Tonry, 1998.

19. D. C. Anderson, 1998; E. Anderson, 1998; Fagan & Wilkinson, 1998; Hagedorn, 1998.

20. Moore & Tonry, 1998, p. 12.

21. Fagan & Wilkinson, 1998.

22. E. Anderson, 1998; Hagedorn, 1998.

23. Fagan & Wilkinson, 1998; Snyder & Sickmund, 1999; Zimring, 1998.

24. Blumstein, 1995.

25. See Howell et al., 1995, p. 10.

26. Wilson, 1995, p. 507.

27. Bennett, DiIulio, & Walters, 1996, p. 27.

28. DiIulio, 1995, 1996.

29. Sickmund et al., 1997; Torbet et al., 1996.

30. Snyder & Sickmund, 1999, p. 103.

31. Zimring, 1998, p. 14.

32. Meddis, 1993.

33. Schwartz, Guo, & Kerbs, 1993.

34. Feiler & Sheley, 1999; Sprott, 1998; Triplett, 1996.

35. Cullen, Fisher, & Applegate, 2000.

36. Bishop, 2000; Bishop & Frazier, 2000; Griffin, Torbet, & Szymanski, 1998.

37. Singer, 2003.

38. Bishop & Frazier, 2000; Forst, Fagan, & Vivona, 1989; Redding, 2003; Reddington & Sapp, 1997.

39. Snyder, 2002; Snyder & Sickmund, 1999.

40. Snyder & Sickmund, 1999, p. 2.

Chapter 2   Separating the Men from the Boys

1. Empey, Stafford, & Hay, 1999.

2. Binder, Geis, & Dickson, 2001, p. 33.

3. Bernard, 1992; Empey et al., 1999.

4. Binder et al., 2001.

5. Bernard, 1992, p. 51.

6. Empey et al., 1999.

7. Empey et al., 1999, p. 25.

8. Binder et al., 2001.

9. Empey et al., 1999.

10. Empey et al., 1999.

11. Sutton, 1988.

12. Bernard, 1992; Binder et al., 2001.

13. Bohm, 2003; Paternoster, 1991.

14. Empey et al., 1999.

15. Binder et al., 2001; Empey et al., 1999.

16. Empey et al., 1999; Feld, 1993; Thomas & Bilchik, 1985.

17. Binder et al., 2001; Empey et al., 1999.

18. Bernard, 1992; Binder et al., 2001.

19. Krisberg & Austin, 1993.

20. Bernard, 1992.

21. Binder et al., 2001, p. 31.

22. Bernard, 1992; Howell, 1997; Krisberg & Austin, 1993.

23. Empey et al., 1999.

24. Bernard, 1992; Howell, 1997; Krisberg & Austin, 1993.

25. Binder et al., 2001; Empey et al., 1999; Thomas & Bilchik, 1985.

26. Howell, 1997.

27. Bernard, 1992, pp. 65–66.

28. Bernard, 1992; Binder et al., 2001; Howell, 1997; Thomas & Bilchik, 1985.

29. Bernard, 1992; Binder et al., 2001; Rendleman, 1979; Thomas & Bilchik, 1985.

30. Empey et al., 1999; Howell, 1997.

31. Krisberg & Austin, 1993.

32. Bernard, 1992.

33. Binder et al., 2001.

34. Bernard, 1992, p. 70.

35. Bernard, 1992; Empey et al., 1999.

36. Empey et al., 1999.

37. Howell, 1997; Krisberg & Austin, 1993.

38. Binder et al., 2001; Howell, 1997; Krisberg & Austin, 1993.

39. Binder et al., 2001; Krisberg & Austin, 1993.

40. Binder et al., 2001; Howell, 1997; Krisberg & Austin, 1993.

41. Krisberg & Austin, 1993, p. 27.

42. Binder et al., 2001; Empey et al., 1999.

43. Bernard, 1992, p. 84.

44. Binder et al., 2001, p. 214.

45. Binder et al., 2001; Empey et al., 1999; Howell, 1997; Krisberg & Austin, 1993.

46. Platt, 1969.

47. Binder et al., 2001.

48. Empey et al., 1999.

49. Bernard, 1992.

50. Bernard, 1992; Thomas & Bilchik, 1985.

51. Feld, 1987, 1993, 1998a, 1998b; Forst & Blomquist, 1991; Howell, 1997.

52. Bernard, 1992, p. 91.

53. Krisberg & Austin, 1993; Thomas & Bilchik, 1985.

54. Binder et al., 2001.

55. Bernard, 1992.

56. Bernard, 1992; Krisberg & Austin, 1993.

57. Empey et al., 1999, p. 47.

58. Feld, 1987, 1993, 1998a, 1998b; Forst & Blomquist, 1991; Howell, 1997, 2003.

59. Thomas & Bilchik, 1985, p. 449.

60. Bernard, 1992.

Chapter 3   Transformation to Criminal

1. Howell, 2003, p. 156.

2. Cable News Network, 1999, 2000; Moore, 2000.

3. Baker, 1979, p. 148.

4. Bernard, 1992; Feld, 1987, 1993, 1998a, 1998b; Forst & Blomquist, 1991; Krisberg & Austin, 1993.

5. Tanenhaus, 2000, p. 19.

6. Rothman, 1980, p. 285.

7. Tanenhaus, 2000.

8. National Council of Juvenile and Family Court Judges, 1998, p. 1.

9. Howell, 2003; Zimring, 1998.

10. Tanenhaus, 2000, p. 27.

11. Tanenhaus, 2000, p. 29.

12. Bernard, 1992; Empey et al., 1999; Thomas & Bilchik, 1985.

13. Forst & Blomquist, 1991.

14. Forst & Blomquist, 1991, p. 328.

15. This concern about the negative effects of labeling in juvenile justice corresponded in time with labeling theory becoming a prominent criminological theory during the 1960s (Binder et al., 2001; Empey et al., 1999).

16. Faust & Brantingham, 1979.

17. *Kent v. United States*, 1966.

18. Faust & Brantingham, 1979, pp. 276–277.

19. Tanenhaus, 2000.

20. Feld, 1987; Frost Clausel & Bonnie, 2000.

21. *In re Gault*, 1967.

22. Faust & Brantingham, 1979, p. 284.

23. Faust & Brantingham, 1979, p. 299.

24. *In re Winship*, 1970.

25. *Breed v. Jones*, 1975.

26. See *McKeiver v. Pennsylvania*, 1971; *Schall v. Martin*, 1984.

27. Forst & Blomquist, 1991, p. 331.

28. Lipton, Martinson, & Wilks, 1975; Martinson, 1974; Sechrest, White, & Brown, 1979.

29. Empey et al., 1999; Forst & Blomquist, 1991; Thomas & Bilchik, 1985.

30. Regnery, 1985, 1986; Wilson, 1983; Wolfgang, 1982.

31. Tonry, 1996, 1998.

32. Feld, 1987, 1993, 1998a, 1998b; Forst & Blomquist, 1991; Thomas & Bilchik, 1985.

33. Snyder & Sickmund, 1995.

34. Blumstein, 1995.

35. Blumstein, 1995; Cook & Laub, 1998; Fagan & Wilkinson, 1998; Greenbaum, 1997; Snyder & Sickmund, 1999.

36. Moore & Tonry, 1998.

37. Sickmund et al., 1997; Torbet et al., 1996; Torbet & Szymanski, 1998.

38. Snyder & Sickmund, 1999.

39. Feld, 1987; Forst & Blomquist, 1991.

40. Krisberg & Austin, 1993; Snyder & Sickmund, 1999.

41. Griffin, 2003.

42. Much has been written about these methods, in a variety of publications (see, for example, Bishop, 2000; Champion & Mays, 1991; Fagan & Zimring, 2000; Feld, 1987, 1993; Forst & Blomquist, 1991; Fritsch & Hemmens, 1995; Griffin, 2003; Griffin et al., 1998; Krisberg & Austin, 1993; Myers, 2001; Sickmund et al., 1997; Snyder & Sickmund, 1995, 1999; Torbet et al., 1996). This section will briefly describe these procedures, with an emphasis on recent reforms and the creation of new transfer strategies in modern times.

43. Dawson, 2000.

44. Griffin, 2003.

45. Torbet et al., 1996; Torbet & Szymanski, 1998.

46. Frost Clausel & Bonnie, 2000.

47. Dawson, 2000; Feld, 2000; Griffin et al., 1998.

48. Feld, 1987, 1993, 1998a, 1998b, 2000.

49. Fagan, 1990; Howell, 1996, 2003; Sanborn, 1994; Zimring, 1991.

50. Dawson, 2000; Griffin, 2003; Griffin et al., 1998.

51. Griffin, 2003.

52. Dawson, 2000, p. 57.

53. Griffin, 2003.

54. Dawson, 2000, p. 59.

55. Griffin, 2003.

56. Frost Clausel & Bonnie, 2000.

57. Feld, 2000, p. 99.

58. Griffin, 2003; Griffin et al., 1998; Torbet et al., 1996; Torbet & Szymanski, 1998.

59. Feld, 2000.

60. Bishop, 2000; Dawson, 2000; Feld, 2000.

61. Sanborn (1994, 2003) has argued that judicial waiver and prosecutorial waiver actually are the only two methods of transfer, as legislative waiver simply extends the power of prosecutors and judges to transfer youths by specifying certain charges to be filed and processed for transfer.

62. Griffin, 2003; Griffin et al., 1998.

63. Feld, 1987, 1993, 1998a, 1998b, 2000.

64. Frost Clausel & Bonnie, 2000; Sanborn, 1994; Singer, 1996.

65. Zimring, 1991, 1998, 2000.

66. Griffin, 2003; Griffin et al., 1998.

67. Griffin, 2003. There are a total of 38 states that generally provide for "automatic transfer" through the use of either legislative waiver or mandatory judicial waiver of certain cases.

68. Torbet et al., 1996; Torbet & Szymanski, 1998.

69. Howell, 1996, 1997, 2003.

70. Griffin, 2003.

71. Griffin, 2003; Griffin et al., 1998.

72. Redding & Howell, 2000; Torbet et al., 1996; Torbet & Szymanski, 1998.

73. Griffin, 2003.

74. Redding & Howell, 2000; Torbet et al., 1996; Torbet & Szymanski, 1998.

75. Griffin, 2003.

76. Griffin, 2003. Great variation exists across states in how and in what combination these criteria are applied (Redding & Howell, 2000).

77. Griffin, 2003; Griffin et al., 1998.

78. Griffin, 2003, p. 12.

79. Howell, 2003, p. 154.

80. Bishop, 2000; Bishop & Frazier, 2000; Howell, 1996, 1997, 2003.

81. Sickmund et al., 1997, p. 31.

82. Puzzanchera, 2003.

83. Howell, 1997, p. 108.

84. Federal Bureau of Investigation, 1997, p. 271.

85. Federal Bureau of Investigation, 2002, p. 291.

86. Snyder & Sickmund (1999, p. 106) reported that in 1996, approximately 218,000 offenders younger than 18 were handled in criminal courts

because under their state law they were deemed to be adults. They were not, however, generally considered to be transferred youth. See also Sickmund et al., 1997.

87. Snyder & Sickmund, 1999, p. 105.

88. Bishop, 2000, p. 108.

89. Bishop, 2000, p. 97.

90. Thomas & Bilchik, 1985.

91. Feld, 1993, 1998a, 1998b.

92. Singer, 1996.

93. Fagan, 1990; Howell, 1997, 2003; Krisberg & Austin, 1993.

94. Myers, 2001.

95. Bell, 1995, 1996a, 1996b.

96. Evanko, 1995, p. A7.

97. Krebs, 1995; Sampson, 1995a, 1995b; Stanley, 1996.

98. Pennsylvania Juvenile Court Judges' Commission, 1992.

99. Feld, 1987, 1993, 1998a, 1998b, 2000.

100. Lemmon, Sontheimer & Saylor, 1991; Myers, 1997.

101. Myers, 2001.

102. Pennsylvania Juvenile Court Judges' Commission, 1996, p. 1.

103. Defined as any firearm, whether loaded or unloaded, or any device designed as a weapon and capable of producing death or serious bodily injury, or any other device or instrumentality which, in the manner in which it is used or intended to be used, is calculated or likely to produce death or serious bodily injury (Crimes Code of Pennsylvania, 2000).

104. Aggravated assault was intentionally omitted from this repeat violent offender clause, apparently based on the belief of policymakers and practitioners that aggravated assault without a deadly weapon could encompass too many violent but less-serious acts (for example, a fist-fight at school).

105. Pennsylvania Juvenile Court Judges' Commission, 1996, pp. 32–34.

Chapter 4   Who Gets Transferred?

1. Myers, 2001; Wolfgang, Figlio, & Sellin, 1972.

2. See, for example, Bishop & Frazier, 1991; Bishop, Frazier, & Henretta, 1989; Bortner, 1986; Champion, 1989; Hamparian et al., 1982; Houghtalin & Mays, 1991; Lemmon et al., 1991; Thomas & Bilchik, 1985.

3. See, for example, Fagan & Deschenes, 1990; Fagan, Forst, & Vivona, 1987; Feld, 1989; Kinder, Veneziano, Fichter, & Azuma, 1995; Myers, 2003c; Podkopacz & Feld, 1996; Poulos & Orchowsky, 1994.

4. Puzzanchera, 2003; Rainville & Smith, 2003; Snyder, Sickmund, & Poe-Yamagata, 2000; Strom, Smith, & Snyder, 1998.

5. Bishop, 2000, p. 110.

6. Singer, 1996; Snyder et al., 2000.

7. Bortner, Zatz, & Hawkins, 2000.

8. See, for example, Clarke, 1996; Clemment, 1997; DeFrances & Strom, 1997; Houghtalin & Mays, 1991; Kinder et al., 1995; Lemmon et al., 1991; Myers, 2001; Puzzanchera, 2003; Rainville & Smith, 2003; Singer, 1996; Snyder et al., 2000; Strom et al., 1998; Thomas & Bilchik, 1985; Torbet, Griffin, Hurst, & MacKenzie, 2000.

9. Snyder & Sickmund, 1999.

10. Eigen, 1981a, 1981b; Keiter, 1973.

11. Fagan & Deschenes, 1990; Fagan et al., 1987; Myers, 2003c; Podkopacz & Feld, 1996; Poulos & Orchowsky, 1994; Singer, 1993. Barnes & Franz (1989), while utilizing fairly strong controls for offense seriousness and prior record, did uncover a significant race effect (that is, nonwhites were more likely to be transferred than whites), although the impact of race was not as substantial as for the legal variables of offense seriousness and prior record. Interestingly, in this study age was not a significant predictor of transfer, but the effect of age was in the expected positive direction.

12. Bortner et al., 2000.

13. Smith, 1986.

14. Leonard, Pope, & Feyerherm, 1995; Myers, 2001; Pope & Feyerherm, 1990; Singer, 1996.

15. Bortner et al., 2000, p. 300.

16. Dawson, 2000, p. 61.

17. See, for example, Clarke, 1996; Houghtalin & Mays, 1991; Kinder et al., 1995; Lemmon et al., 1991; Myers, 2001; Poulos & Orchowsky, 1994; Singer, 1996; Thomas & Bilchik, 1985.

18. DeFrances & Strom, 1997; Puzzanchera, 2003; Rainville & Smith, 2003; Snyder et al., 2000; Strom et al., 1998.

19. For a good example of research on transferred female offenders, see the qualitative study by Gaarder and Belknap (2002). Their in-depth interviews with 22 waived and incarcerated female teenagers revealed significant histories of violence, victimization, sexism, racism, and economic marginalization.

20. Feld, 1989; Hamparian et al., 1982; Poulos & Orchowsky, 1994; Torbet et al., 2000.

21. Bishop & Frazier, 1991; Bishop et al., 1989; Bortner, 1986; Champion, 1989; Hamparian et al., 1982; Lemmon et al., 1991; Thomas & Bilchik, 1985.

22. Snyder & Sickmund, 1995.

23. DeFrances & Strom, 1997; Howell, 1997; Sickmund et al., 1997.

24. Puzzanchera, 2003.

25. Bishop, 2000; Myers, 2001; Rainville & Smith, 2003; Snyder et al., 2000; Strom et al., 1998.

26. Barnes & Franz, 1989; Fagan et al., 1987; Kinder et al., 1995; Poulos & Orchowsky, 1994.

27. Fagan & Deschenes, 1990; Lee, 1994; Myers, 2003c; Podkopacz & Feld, 1996.

28. Barnes & Franz, 1989; Lee, 1994; Myers, 2003c; Podkopacz & Feld, 1996; Poulos & Orchowsky, 1994.

29. Fagan & Deschenes, 1990; Fagan et al., 1987.

30. Dawson, 2000, p. 60.

31. Poulos & Orchowsky, 1994.

32. Podkopacz & Feld, 1996.

33. Podkopacz & Feld, 1996, p. 478.

34. Podkopacz & Feld, 1996, p. 479.

35. See also Myers, 2003c.

36. Fagan, 1990; Howell, 1996, 2003; Sanborn, 1994; Zimring, 1991, 1998, 2000.

37. Feld, 1987, 1993, 1998a, 1998b, 2000; Podkopacz & Feld, 1996.

38. Bennett et al., 1996; DiIulio, 1995, 1996.

39. Bishop, 2000, pp. 124–125.

40. Bishop, 2000; Bishop & Frazier, 2000; Frost Clausel & Bonnie, 2000.

41. Torbet et al., 2000; Zimring, 1991, 1998, 2000.

42. Bishop, 2000, p. 125.

43. Griffin, 2003; Torbet et al., 2000.

44. Fried & Reppucci, 2001; Geraghty, 1998; Morse, 1998; Scott & Grisso, 1998; Steinberg & Cauffman, 1996.

45. Bishop, 2000; Torbet et al., 2000; Young, 2000.

46. Singer, 1996.

47. Snyder et al., 2000.

48. Snyder et al., 2000, p. 38.

49. In my research (Myers, 2001) examining judicial waivers of violent youths processed in Pennsylvania in 1994, I found that 25% of the 557 offenders in the study were transferred to adult court, and of these 138 youths, 87% were convicted in adult court. These figures support the findings and conclusions of Snyder et al. (2000) and suggest that the juvenile court was successful in waiving the "most deserving" offenders who later experienced a high likelihood of conviction in criminal court.

50. Cable News Network, 1999, 2000; Moore, 2000.

51. Howell, 2003, p. 156.

52. Bishop, 2000; Bishop & Frazier, 2000.

53. Cable News Network, 1999.

54. Moore, 2000, pp. 6–7.

55. Jones & Roberts, 1998.

56. Howell, 2003; Moore, 2000.

57. Moore, 2000, p. 7.

58. Jones & Roberts, 1998.

59. Howell, 2003.

60. Moore, 2000, p. 10.

Chapter 5   What Happens in Adult Court?

1. Feld, 1993, 1998a, 1998b; Greenwood, 1995; Krisberg & Austin, 1993; Moore & Wakeling, 1997; Schwartz, 1989.

2. Fagan, 1995; Feld, 1993; Singer, 1996.

3. Greenwood, 1995.

4. Sickmund et al., 1997; Torbet et al., 1996; Torbet & Szymanski, 1998.

5. See, for example, Bartol & Bartol, 1998; Binder et al., 2001; Elrod & Ryder, 1999.

6. Strom et al., 1998.

7. Only 13% of the murder defendants were released compared with about half of those charged with rape, robbery, and assault.

8. Rainville & Smith, 2003. Only 10% of the murder defendants were released.

9. Myers, 2001; Myers & Kiehl, 2001.

10. Bishop, 2000; Bishop & Frazier, 2000; Bishop, Frazier, Lanza-Kaduce, & White, 1999.

11. Fagan & Guggenheim, 1996.

12. Bortner & Reed, 1985; Clarke & Koch, 1980; Dannefer, 1984; Feld, 1988; Frazier & Cochran, 1986; Myers, 2003a.

13. Bishop & Frazier, 1991; Bishop et al., 1989; Bortner, 1986; Champion, 1989; Clarke, 1996; Clemment, 1997; Eigen, 1981a, 1981b; Fagan, 1990; Gillespie & Norman, 1984; Hamparian et al., 1982; Houghtalin & Mays, 1991; Lemmon et al., 1991; Myers, 2001; Podkopacz & Feld, 1996; Rainville & Smith, 2003; Rudman, Hartstone, Fagan, & Moore, 1986; Snyder et al., 2000; Strom et al., 1998; Thomas & Bilchik, 1985. For exceptions, see Kinder et al., 1995; Sagatun, McCollum, & Edwards, 1985; Singer, 1996.

14. Eigen, 1981a, 1981b.

15. Rudman et al., 1986.

16. Rudman et al., 1986, pp. 86–87.

17. Fagan, 1990; Fagan & Deschenes, 1990; Fagan et al., 1987.

18. Fagan, 1990, p. 114.

19. Myers, 2001, 2003a.

20. Kinder et al., 1995.

21. Fagan, 1995.

22. See also Singer, 1996.

23. Fagan, 1995, p. 253.

24. Podkopacz & Feld, 1996.

25. Podkopacz & Feld, 1996, p. 485, note 98.

26. See also Strom et al., 1998.

27. Singer, 1996; Snyder et al., 2000.

28. Bortner, 1986; Champion, 1989; Emerson, 1981; Gillespie & Norman, 1984; Hamparian et al., 1982; Royscher & Edelman, 1981; Sagatun et al., 1985.

29. Hagan & Bumiller, 1983.

30. Barnes & Franz, 1989; Bishop, 2000; Bishop & Frazier, 1991, 2000; Bishop et al., 1989; Bortner, 1986; Champion, 1989; Hamparian et al., 1982; Podkopacz & Feld, 1996; Rainville & Smith, 2003; Strom et al., 1998.

31. Barnes & Franz, 1989; Bishop, 2000; Bishop & Frazier, 2000; Clarke, 1996; Eigen, 1981a, 1981b; Fagan, 1990, 1995; Houghtalin & Mays, 1991; Myers, 2001, 2003a; Podkopacz & Feld, 1996; Rainville & Smith, 2003; Rudman et al., 1986; Strom et al., 1998.

32. Eigen, 1981a, 1981b.

33. Rudman et al., 1986.

34. Fagan, 1990.

35. Myers, 2001, 2003a.

36. Barnes & Franz, 1989.

37. Fagan, 1995.

38. Podkopacz & Feld, 1996.

39. Podkopacz & Feld, 1996, p. 487.

40. Bishop, Frazier, Lanza-Kaduce, & Winner, 1996.

41. Podkopacz & Feld, 1996, p. 487.

42. See, for example, Bishop, 2000; Bishop & Frazier, 1991; Bishop et al., 1989; Clemment, 1997; Lemmon et al., 1991; Myers, 2001; Rainville & Smith, 2003; Singer, 1996; Thomas & Bilchik, 1985.

43. Eigen, 1981a, 1981b.

44. Rudman et al., 1986.

45. Fagan, 1990.

46. Bishop et al., 1996.

47. Myers, 2001, 2003a.

48. Snyder & Sickmund, 1999, p. 93.

49. Podkopacz & Feld, 1996.

50. Fagan, 1995.

51. Fritsch, Caeti, & Hemmens, 1996.

52. Butts, 1996, 1997; Butts & Halemba, 1994.

53. Howell, 1997; Krisberg, Currie, Onek, & Wiebush, 1995.

54. Butts, 1997.

55. Lemmon et al., 1991.

56. Kinder et al., 1995.

57. Rudman et al., 1986.

58. Fagan, 1995.

59. Myers, 2001, 2003c.

Chapter 6   Prospects for Punishment and Rehabilitation

1. Allen & Simonsen, 2001; Binder et al., 2001; Empey et al., 1999; Howell, 1997; Silverman, 2001.

2. Gibbons, 1999.

3. Tonry, 1996, 1998.

4. Binder et al., 2001; Empey et al., 1999; Howell, 1997.

5. Conley, 1994, pp. ix–x.

6. President's Commission on Law Enforcement and Administration of Justice, 1967.

7. Conley, 1994; Tonry, 1998.

8. Reiss, 1994.

9. Stojkovic, 1994.

10. Pisciotta, 1994.

11. Moore & Tonry, 1998; Myers, 2001.

12. Tonry, 1998.

13. Tonry, 1998.

14. Tonry, 1996.

15. Lipton et al., 1975; Martinson, 1974.

16. Sechrest et al., 1979.

17. Tonry, 1998.

18. Harrison & Karberg, 2004.

19. Tonry, 1996, 1998.

20. Sherman, Farrington, Welsh, & MacKenzie, 2002; Tonry, 1998.

21. MacKenzie, 2002.

22. Applegate & Cullen, 1997; Butts & Mears, 2001; Cullen, Latessa, Burton, & Lombardo, 1993; Gibbons, 1999.

23. Andrews et al., 1990; Gaes, 1998; Gendreau, Little, & Goggin, 1996; Gendreau & Ross, 1987.

24. MacKenzie, 2002.

25. Gendreau, Goggin, & Smith, 1999.

26. Andrews et al., 1990, p. 374.

27. MacKenzie, 2002.

28. Pisciotta, 1994.

29. President's Commission on Law Enforcement and Administration of Justice, 1967.

30. Pisciotta, 1994, p. 87.

31. Wilson, 1975.

32. Regnery, 1985, 1986; Wilson, 1983; Wolfgang, 1982.

33. Pisciotta, 1994.

34. Lab & Whitehead, 1988; Whitehead & Lab, 1989.

35. Sickmund et al., 1997; Snyder & Sickmund, 1995; Torbet et al., 1996.

36. Farrington et al., 1986; Howell, 1996, 1997; Myers, 2001.

37. Bennett et al., 1996; DiIulio, 1995, 1996; Wilson, 1995.

38. Butts & Mears, 2001; Gibbons, 1999; Howell, 1997, 2003; Howell et al., 1995; Krisberg & Austin, 1993; Lipsey, 1992, 1995; Loeber & Farrington, 1999; Sherman et al., 1997, 2002.

39. Snyder, 2002; Snyder & Sickmund, 1999.

40. Austin, Dedel Johnson, & Gregoriou, 2000; Snyder & Sickmund, 1999.

41. Snyder & Sickmund, 1999.

42. Feld, 1993, 1998b; Parent, Leiter, Livens, Wentworth, & Stephen, 1994; Redding, 2003; Smith, 1998.

43. Feld, 1993, p. 251.

44. Howell, 2003.

45. Lipsey, 1992, 1995, 1999; Lipsey & Wilson, 1999.

46. Andrews et al., 1990; Gaes, 1998; Gendreau, et al., 1996; MacKenzie, 2002.

47. Austin et al., 2000.

48. Bishop, 2000; Bishop & Frazier, 2000.

49. Howell, 2003; Lipsey & Wilson, 1999; MacKenzie, 2002.

50. Bishop, 2000; Bishop & Frazier, 2000.

51. Flaherty, 1980; Forst et al., 1989; Redding, 2003.

52. Bishop, 2000; Bishop & Frazier, 2000.

53. Reddington & Sapp, 1997.

54. Austin et al., 2000; Bishop, 2000; Bishop & Frazier, 2000; Myers, 2001; Redding, 2003.

55. Redding, 2003, pp. 141–142.

56. Austin et al., 2000; Redding, 2003.

57. Zimmerman et al., 2000.

58. Myers, 2003b, 2003c.

59. Erdley, 2002; Wells, 2002; White Stack, 2001.

60. Hartman, 2003.

61. Singer, 1996; Snyder et al., 2000.

62. Erdley, 2002; Wells, 2002.

63. Snyder et al., 2000.

64. Hartman, 2003.

Chapter 7 General and Specific Deterrence

1. Wilson, 1995, p. 494.

2. Bishop et al., 1996.

3. Fagan, 1995.

4. Beccaria, 1764/1986.

5. Beccaria, 1764/1986, p. 36.

6. Beccaria, 1764/1986, p. 46.

7. Beccaria, 1764/1986, p. 46.

8. Andenaes, 1974; Blumstein, Cohen, & Nagin, 1978; Gibbs, 1975; Nagin, 1998; Paternoster, 1987; Zimring & Hawkins, 1973.

9. Wilson, 1995.

10. Gibbs, 1975; Nagin, 1998; Paternoster, 1987; Zimring & Hawkins, 1973.

11. "The purpose of punishment, then, is nothing other than to dissuade the criminal from doing fresh harm to his compatriots and to keep other people from doing the same" (Beccaria, 1764/1986, p. 23).

12. Andenaes, 1968, p. 78.

13. Nagin, 1978, p. 96.

14. Stafford & Warr, 1993.

15. Nagin, 1978; Paternoster, 1987.

16. Chiricos & Waldo, 1970; Gibbs, 1968, 1975; Logan, 1975; Tittle, 1969; Tittle & Rowe, 1974; Zimring & Hawkins, 1973.

17. Paternoster, 1987.

18. Minor & Harry, 1982; Paternoster, Saltzman, Chiricos, & Waldo, 1982; Paternoster, Saltzman, Waldo, & Chiricos, 1983; Saltzman, Paternoster, Waldo, & Chiricos, 1982.

19. Paternoster, 1989b; Paternoster & Iovanni, 1986; Paternoster et al., 1983; Piliavin, Gartner, Thorton, & Matsueda, 1986.

20. Paternoster, 1987.

21. Klepper & Nagin, 1989.

22. Nagin, 1998.

23. Bachman, Paternoster, & Ward, 1992; Grasmick & Bursik, 1990; Klepper & Nagin, 1989; Nagin & Paternoster, 1993; Piquero & Tibbetts, 1996.

24. Nagin, 1998.

25. Andenaes, 1968.

26. Paternoster & Piquero, 1995, p. 251; see also DeJong, 1997; Gibbs, 1975; Paternoster, 1989a.

27. Gibbs, 1975; Paternoster, 1989b.

28. Sherman, 1993; Smith & Gartin, 1989.

29. Becker, 1963; Lemert, 1951, 1972; Tannenbaum, 1938.

30. Paternoster & Iovanni, 1989; Thomas & Bishop, 1984.

31. Smith & Paternoster, 1990, pp. 1109–1110.

32. Smith & Paternoster, 1990, pp. 1111–1112.

33. Farrington, 1983.

34. Smith & Paternoster, 1990; but see Bishop et al., 1996, for an exception.

35. Because juvenile transfer focuses on the punishment of youthful offenders, the following discussion will center on research directed at this target population. For broader reviews of research on specific deterrence and labeling effects, see Farrington (1983), Gibbs (1975), Mahoney (1974), Paternoster & Iovanni (1989), Sherman (1993), Sherman et al. (2002), Wilson (1983), and Zimring & Hawkins (1973).

36. Gold & Williams, 1969.

37. Klemke, 1978.

38. Smith & Gartin, 1989.

39. Smith & Gartin, 1989, p. 103.

40. Paternoster & Piquero, 1995.

41. Stafford & Warr, 1993.

42. Empey & Erickson, 1972.

43. Empey et al., 1999.

44. Maltz, 1984; Wooldredge, 1988.

45. Murray & Cox, 1979.

46. Klein, 1986.

47. Wooldredge, 1988.

48. Wooldredge, 1988, p. 293.

49. Schneider & Ervin, 1990.

50. Schneider & Ervin, 1990.

51. Gottfredson & Barton, 1993.

52. Gottfredson & Barton, 1993, p. 604.

53. Coates, Miller, & Ohlin, 1978.

54. Krisberg, Austin, & Steele, 1989.

55. Brown, Miller, & Jenkins, 1987; Brown, Miller, Jenkins, & Rhodes, 1989; Brown, Miller, Jenkins, & Rhodes, 1991.

56. Jacobs, 1990.

57. Minor, Hartmann, & Terry, 1997.

58. Minor et al., 1997, pp. 341–342.

59. Smith & Gartin, 1989.

60. Jacobs, 1990; Klein, 1986; Minor et al., 1997; Wooldredge, 1988.

61. Gottfredson & Barton, 1993; Murray & Cox, 1979.

62. Farrington, 1977; Farrington, Osborn, & West, 1978; Shannon, 1980; Wolfgang et al., 1972.

63. Smith & Gartin, 1989, p. 103.

64. Singer & McDowall, 1988; see also Singer, 1996.

65. Jensen & Metsger, 1994.

66. Risler, Sweatman, & Nackerud, 1998.

67. Levitt, 1998.

68. Redding, 2003.

69. Fagan, 1995.

70. Bishop et al., 1996.

71. Winner, Lanza-Kaduce, Bishop, & Frazier, 1997.

72. Podkopacz & Feld, 1996.

73. Myers, 2001, 2003c; Myers & Kiehl, 2001.

74. Sherman, 1993.

75. Lanza-Kaduce & Radosevich, 1987; Makkai & Braithwaite, 1994; Paternoster, Brame, Bachman, & Sherman, 1997; Tyler, 1990.

76. Sherman, 1992; Sherman & Smith, 1992.

77. Sherman, 1993.

78. Empey et al., 1999.

79. Paternoster & Piquero, 1995, pp. 270–271.

Chapter 8   The Rise and Fall of "Adult Crime, Adult Time"

1. Cook & Laub, 1998; Moore & Tonry, 1998; Snyder & Sickmund, 1999; Zimring, 1998.

2. Snyder, 2002; Snyder & Sickmund, 1999.

3. Smalley, 2004.

4. Jonas, 2004

5. Jonas, 2004, p. 2.

6. Johnson, 2004.

7. Johnson, 2004, pp. 1A–2A.

8. Snyder & Sickmund, 1999, p. 2.

9. Fried & Reppucci, 2001; Morse, 1998; Scott & Grisso, 1998; Steinberg & Cauffman, 1996.

10. Steinberg & Cauffman, 1996, p. 268.

11. Redding, 2003.

12. Myers, 2001.

13. Myers, 2001, p. 178.

14. Howell, 1997, 2003; Howell et al., 1995; Krisberg & Austin, 1993; Loeber & Farrington, 1999.

15. Hawkins, Arthur, & Catalano, 1995; Hawkins et al., 1999; Howell, 2003; Lipsey & Derzon, 1999; Loeber & Farrington, 1999.

16. Office of Juvenile Justice and Delinquency Prevention, 2002.

17. Howell, 2003.

18. Catalano, Arthur, Hawkins, Berglund, & Olson, 1999; Developmental Research and Programs, Inc., 1997, 1998; Howell, 2003; Wong, Catalano, Hawkins, & Chappell, 1996.

19. Greenberg & Feinberg, 2002.

20. Krisberg et al., 1995, pp. 153–154.

21. Howell, 2003, p. 224.

22. Blumstein et al., 1986; Farrington, 1986, 1998; Loeber & LeBlanc, 1990; Myers, 2001; Thornberry, Huizinga, & Loeber, 1995.

23. Howell, 1997, 2003; Howell et al., 1995.

24. Howell, 2003, pp. 251–257.

25. Feld, 1993, 1998a, 1998b.

26. Moore & Wakeling, 1997.

27. Feld, 1998a, p. 133.

28. Moore & Wakeling, 1997.

29. *Eddings v. Oklahoma*, 455 U.S. 104, 1982; *Stanford v. Kentucky*, 492 U.S. 361, 1989; *Thompson v. Oklahoma*, 487 U.S. 815, 1988; *Wilkins v. Missouri*, 492 U.S. 361, 1989.

30. Wilson, 2000.

31. Bonczar & Snell, 2003.

32. Wilson, 2000.

33. Austin et al., 2001; Paternoster, 1991.

34. Bonczar & Snell, 2003.

35. Austin et al., 2001; Paternoster, 1991.

36. Bonczar & Snell, 2003.

37. Austin et al., 2001.

38. Vogel & Vogel, 2003.

39. "Missouri court," 2003.

40. *State ex rel. Christopher Simmons v. Roper*, SC84454, 2003.

41. *Atkins v. Virginia*, 536 U.S. 304, 2002.

42. *Roper v. Simmons*, 124 S. Ct. 1171, 2004.

43. Bishop, 2000; Bishop & Frazier, 2000; Myers, 2001.

44. Blumstein, 1995; Cook & Laub, 1998; Fagan & Wilkinson, 1998; Greenbaum, 1997.

45. Sickmund et al., 1997.

46. Myers, 2001, 2003a, 2003b, 2003c; Myers & Kiehl, 2001.

47. Myers, 2001.

48. Myers, 2001.

49. Blumstein et al., 1986; Farrington et al., 1986; Feld, 1998a, 1998b.

50. Griffin, 2003.

51. Feld, 1989; Zimring, 1991.

52. Sickmund, 2003.

53. Blumstein, 1988, 1995; Blumstein et al., 1986; Farrington, 1986, 1998.

54. Griffin, 2003.

55. Gottfredson & Barton, 1993; Murray & Cox, 1979; Myers, 2001.

Bibliography

Allen, H. E., & Simonsen, C. E. (2001). *Corrections in America: An introduction* (9th ed.). Upper Saddle River, NJ: Prentice Hall.

Andenaes, J. (1968). Does punishment deter crime? *Criminal Law Quarterly, 11,* 76–93.

Andenaes, J. (1974). *Punishment and deterrence.* Ann Arbor, MI: University of Michigan Press.

Anderson, D. C. (1998). Curriculum, culture, and community: The challenge of school violence. In M. Tonry & M. H. Moore (Eds.), *Crime and justice: A review of research* (Vol. 24, pp. 317–363). Chicago: The University of Chicago Press.

Anderson, E. (1998). The social ecology of youth violence. In M. Tonry & M. H. Moore (Eds.), *Crime and justice: A review of research* (Vol. 24, pp. 65–104). Chicago: The University of Chicago Press.

Andrews, D. A., Zinger, I., Hodge, R. D., Bonta, J., Gendreau, P., & Cullen, F. T. (1990). Does correctional treatment work? A clinically relevant and psychologically informed meta-analysis. *Criminology, 28,* 369–404.

Applegate, B. K., & Cullen, F. T. (1997). Public support for correctional treatment: The continuing appeal of the rehabilitative ideal. *Prison Journal, 77*(3), 237–259.

Atkins v. Virginia, 536 U.S. 304 (2002).

Austin, J., Calavita, K., Chilton, R., Fagan, J., Johnson, C. C., Jones-Brown, D., et al. (2001, November). *The use of the death penalty.* Paper presented at the annual meeting of the American Society of Criminology, Atlanta, GA.

Austin, J., Dedel Johnson, K., & Gregoriou, M. (2000). *Juveniles in adult prisons and jails* (Report No. NCJ 182503). Washington, DC: U.S. Department of Justice.

Bachman, R., Paternoster, R., & Ward, S. (1992). The rationality of sexual offending: Testing a deterrence/rational choice conception of sexual assault. *Law & Society Review, 26*(2), 343–372.

Baker, H. H. (1979). Procedure of the Boston juvenile court. In F. L. Faust & P. J. Brantingham (Eds.), *Juvenile justice philosophy: Readings, cases, and comments* (2nd ed., pp. 146–155). St. Paul, MN: West Publishing.

Barnes, C. W., & Franz, R. S. (1989). Questionably adult: Determinants and effects of the juvenile waiver decision. *Justice Quarterly, 6*(1), 117–135.

Bartol, C. R., & Bartol, A. M. (1998). *Delinquency and justice: A psychosocial approach.* Englewood Cliffs, NJ: Prentice Hall.

Beccaria, C. (1764/1986). *On crimes and punishments.* Indianapolis, IN: Hackett Publishing.

Becker, H. S. (1963). *Outsiders.* New York: Free Press.

Bell, A. (1995, May 11). Bill highlights "public safety." *The Patriot-News,* p. B1.

Bell, A. (1996a, February 4). Funding plummets while juvenile crime escalates: $45 million loss may prompt lawsuit. *Sunday Patriot-News,* p. B1.

Bell, A. (1996b, February 1). Juvenile system direction said needed: State pays out $400 million for underage crime programs. *The Patriot-News,* p. B6.

Bennett, W. J., DiIulio, J. J., & Walters, J. P. (1996). *Body count: Moral poverty. . . And how to win America's war against crime and drugs.* New York: Simon & Schuster.

Bernard, T. J. (1992). *The cycle of juvenile justice.* New York: Oxford University Press.

Binder, A., Geis, G., & Dickson, B. D., Jr. (2001). *Juvenile delinquency: Historical, cultural, and legal perspectives* (3rd ed.). Cincinnati, OH: Anderson Publishing Co.

Bishop, D. M. (2000). Juvenile offenders in the adult criminal justice system. In M. Tonry (Ed.), *Crime and justice: A review of research* (Vol. 27, pp. 81–167). Chicago: The University of Chicago Press.

Bishop, D. M., & Frazier, C. E. (1991). Transfer of juveniles to criminal court: A case study and analysis of prosecutorial waiver. *Notre Dame Journal of Law, Ethics & Public Policy, 5,* 281–302.

Bishop, D. M., & Frazier, C. E. (2000). Consequences of transfer. In J. Fagan & F. Zimring (Eds.), *The changing borders of juvenile justice: Transfer of adolescents to the criminal court* (pp. 227–276). Chicago: The University of Chicago Press.

Bishop, D. M., Frazier, C. E., & Henretta, J. C. (1989). Prosecutorial waiver: Case study of a questionable reform. *Crime & Delinquency, 35*(2), 179–201.

Bishop, D. M., Frazier, C. E., Lanza-Kaduce, L., & White, G. H. (1999). *A study of juvenile transfers to criminal court in Florida* (Report No. FS-99113). Washington, DC: Office of Juvenile Justice and Delinquency Prevention.

Bishop, D. M., Frazier, C. E., Lanza-Kaduce, L., & Winner, L. (1996). The transfer of juveniles to criminal court: Does it make a difference? *Crime & Delinquency, 42*(2), 171–191.

Blumstein, A. (1988). Prison populations: A system out of control? In M. Tonry (Ed.), *Crime and justice: An annual review of research* (Vol. 10, pp. 231–265). Chicago: The University of Chicago Press.

Blumstein, A. (1995). Youth violence, guns, and the illicit-drug industry. *The Journal of Criminal Law and Criminology, 86*(1), 10–36.

Blumstein, A., Cohen, J., & Nagin, D. (1978). *Deterrence and incapacitation: Estimating the effects of criminal sanctions on crime rates.* Washington, DC: National Academy of Sciences.

Blumstein, A., Cohen, J., Roth, J., & Visher, C. (1986). *Criminal careers and "career criminals."* Washington, DC: National Academy Press.

Bohm, R. (2003). *Deathquest: An introduction to the theory and practice of capital punishment in the United States* (2nd ed.). Cincinnati, OH: Anderson Publishing.

Bonczar, T. P., & Snell, T. L. (2003). *Capital punishment, 2002* (Report No. NCJ 201848). Washington, DC: Bureau of Justice Statistics.

Bortner, M. A. (1986). Traditional rhetoric, organizational realities: Remand of juveniles to adult court. *Crime & Delinquency, 32*(1), 53–73.

Bortner, M. A., & Reed, W. L. (1985). The preeminence of process: An example of refocused justice research. *Social Science Quarterly, 66,* 413–425.

Bortner, M. A., Zatz, M. S., & Hawkins, D. F. (2000). Race and transfer: Empirical research and social context. In J. Fagan & F. E. Zimring (Eds.), *The changing borders of juvenile justice: Transfer of adolescents to the criminal court* (pp. 277–320). Chicago: The University of Chicago Press.

Breed v. Jones, 421 U.S. 519 (1975).

Brown, W. K., Miller, T. P., & Jenkins, R. L. (1987). The favorable effect of juvenile court adjudication of delinquent youth on the first contact with the juvenile justice system. *Juvenile and Family Court Journal, 38*, 21–26.

Brown, W. K., Miller, T. P., Jenkins, R. L., & Rhodes, W. A. (1989). The effect of early juvenile court adjudication on adult outcomes. *International Journal of Offender Therapy and Comparative Criminology, 33*, 177–183.

Brown, W. K., Miller, T. P., Jenkins, R. L., & Rhodes, W. A. (1991). The human costs of "Giving the kid another chance." *International Journal of Offender Therapy and Comparative Criminology, 35*(4), 296–302.

Butts, J. A. (1996). Speedy trial in the juvenile court. *American Journal of Criminal Law, 23*, 515–560.

Butts, J. A. (1997). Necessarily relative: Is juvenile justice speedy enough? *Crime & Delinquency, 43*(1), 3–23.

Butts, J. A., & Halemba, G. J. (1994). Delays in juvenile justice: Findings from a national survey. *Juvenile and Family Court Journal, 45*, 31–46.

Butts, J. A., & Mears, D. P. (2001). Reviving juvenile justice in a get-tough era. *Youth & Society, 33*(2), 169–198.

Cable News Network. (1999, October 29). *Prosecutor: Boy, 11, bragged he'd kill, then did.* Retrieved July 25, 2003, from http://www.cnn.com.

Cable News Network. (2000, January 13). *Michigan judge sentences boy killer to juvenile detention.* Retrieved July 25, 2003, from http://www.cnn.com.

Catalano, R. F., Arthur, M. W., Hawkins, J. D., Berglund, L., & Olson, J. J. (1999). Comprehensive community- and school-based interventions to prevent antisocial behavior. In R. Loeber & D. P. Farrington (Eds.), *Serious and violent juvenile offenders: Risk factors and successful interventions* (pp. 248–283). Thousand Oaks, CA: Sage Publications.

Champion, D. J. (1989). Teenage felons and waiver hearings: Some recent trends, 1980–1988. *Crime & Delinquency, 35*(4), 577–585.

Champion, D. J., & Mays, G. L. (1991). *Transferring juveniles to criminal courts: Trends and implications for criminal justice.* New York: Praeger Publishers.

Chiricos, T. G., & Waldo, G. P. (1970). Punishment and crime: An examination of some empirical evidence. *Social Problems, 18*, 200–217.

Clarke, E. E. (1996). A case for reinventing juvenile transfer. *Juvenile and Family Court Journal, 47*, 3–22.

Clarke, S. H., & Koch, G. G. (1980). Juvenile court: Therapy or crime control, and do lawyers make a difference? *Law & Society Review, 14*, 263–308.

Clemment, M. J. (1997). A five-year study of juvenile waiver and adult sentences: Implications for policy. *Criminal Justice Policy Review, 8*(2 & 3), 201–219.

Coates, R. B., Miller, A. B., & Ohlin, L. E. (1978). *Diversity in a youth correctional system: Handling delinquents in Massachusetts.* Cambridge, MA: Ballinger.

Conley, J. A. (1994). *The 1967 President's Crime Commission Report: Its impact 25 years later.* Cincinnati, OH: Anderson Publishing.

Cook, P. J., & Laub, J. H. (1998). The unprecedented epidemic in youth violence. In M. Tonry & M. H. Moore (Eds.), *Crime and justice: A review of research* (Vol. 24, pp. 27–64). Chicago: The University of Chicago Press.

Crimes Code of Pennsylvania, 18 PA C.S. Sec. 2301 (2000). Binghamton, NY: Gould.

Cullen, F. T., Fisher, B. S., & Applegate, B. K. (2000). Public opinion about punishment and corrections. In M. Tonry (Ed.), *Crime and justice: A review of research* (Vol. 27, pp. 1–79). Chicago: The University of Chicago Press.

Cullen, F. T., Latessa, E. J., Burton, V. S., Jr., & Lombardo, L. X. (1993). The correctional orientation of prison wardens: Is the rehabilitative ideal supported? *Criminology, 31*(1), 69–92.

Dannefer, D. (1984). Who signs the complaint? Relation distance and the juvenile justice process. *Law & Society Review, 18*, 249–271.

Dawson, R. O. (2000). Judicial waiver in theory and practice. In J. Fagan & F. E. Zimring (Eds.), *The changing borders of juvenile justice: Transfer of adolescents to the criminal court* (pp. 45–81). Chicago: The University of Chicago Press.

DeFrances, C. J., & Strom, K. J. (1997). *Juveniles prosecuted in state criminal courts* (Report No. NCJ 164265). Washington, DC: Bureau of Justice Statistics/ Office of Juvenile Justice and Delinquency Prevention.

DeJong, C. (1997). Survival analysis and specific deterrence: Integrating theoretical and empirical models of recidivism. *Criminology, 35*(4), 561–575.

Developmental Research and Programs, Inc. (1997). *Communities That Care: Promising approaches.* Seattle, WA: Developmental Research and Programs, Inc.

Developmental Research and Programs, Inc. (1998). *Communities That Care.* Seattle, WA: Developmental Research and Programs, Inc.

DiIulio, J. J. (1995, November 27). The coming of the super-predators. *Weekly Standard*, pp. 23–28.

DiIulio, J. J. (1996, Spring). They're coming: Florida's youth crime bomb. *Impact*, pp. 25–27.

Eddings v. Oklahoma, 455 U.S. 104 (1982).

Eigen, J. P. (1981a). The determinants and impact of jurisdictional transfer in Philadelphia. In J. C. Hall, D. M. Hamparian, J. M. Pettibone, & J. L. White (Eds.), *Major issues in juvenile justice information and training: Readings in public policy* (pp. 333–350). Columbus, OH: Academy for Contemporary Problems.

Eigen, J. P. (1981b). Punishing youth homicide offenders in Philadelphia. *The Journal of Criminal Law and Criminology, 72*(3), 1072–1093.

Elrod, P., & Ryder, P. S. (1999). *Juvenile justice: A social, historical, and legal perspective.* Gaithersburg, MD: Aspen.

Emerson, R. (1981). On last resorts. *American Journal of Sociology, 87,* 1–22.

Empey, L. T., & Erickson, M. L. (1972). *The Provo experiment: Evaluating community control of delinquency.* Lexington, MA: D. C. Heath.

Empey, L. T., Stafford, M. C., & Hay, C. H. (1999). *American delinquency: Its meaning & construction* (4th ed.). Belmont, CA: Wadsworth Publishing Company.

Erdley, D. (2002, April 14). Pine Grove: Experimental juvenile prison built for a crime wave that didn't happen. *Pittsburgh Sunday Tribune Review,* pp. A1, A12.

Evanko, P. J. (1995, August 28). Violent juvenile crime is growing state problem. *The Patriot-News,* p. A7.

Fagan, J. (1990). Social and legal policy dimensions of violent juvenile crime. *Criminal Justice and Behavior, 17*(1), 93–133.

Fagan, J. (1995). Separating the men from the boys: The comparative advantage of juvenile versus criminal court sanctions on recidivism among adolescent felony offenders. In J. C. Howell, B. Krisberg, J. D. Hawkins, & J. J. Wilson (Eds.), *A sourcebook: Serious, violent, & chronic juvenile offenders* (pp. 238–260). Thousand Oaks, CA: Sage Publications.

Fagan, J., & Deschenes, E. P. (1990). Determinants of judicial waiver decisions for violent juvenile offenders. *The Journal of Criminal Law and Criminology, 81*(2), 314–347.

Fagan, J., Forst, M., & Vivona, T. S. (1987). Racial determinants of the judicial transfer decision: Prosecuting violent youth in criminal court. *Crime & Delinquency, 33*(2), 259–286.

Fagan, J., & Guggenheim, M. (1996). Preventive detention and the judicial prediction of dangerousness for juveniles: A natural experiment. *The Journal of Criminal Law and Criminology, 86*(2), 415–488.

Fagan, J., & Wilkinson, D. L. (1998). Guns, youth violence, and social identity in inner cities. In M. Tonry & M. H. Moore (Eds.), *Crime and justice: A review of research* (Vol. 24, pp. 105–188). Chicago: The University of Chicago Press.

Fagan, J., & Zimring, F. E. (2000). *The changing borders of juvenile justice: Transfer of adolescents to the criminal court.* Chicago: The University of Chicago Press.

Farrington, D. P. (1977). The effects of public labelling. *British Journal of Criminology, 17*(2), 112–125.

Farrington, D. P. (1983). Randomized experiments in crime and justice. In M. Tonry & N. Morris (Eds.), *Crime and justice: An annual review of research* (Vol. 4, pp. 257–308). Chicago: The University of Chicago Press.

Farrington, D. P. (1986). Age and crime. In M. Tonry & N. Morris (Eds.), *Crime and justice: An annual review of research* (Vol. 7, pp. 189–250). Chicago: The University of Chicago Press.

Farrington, D. P. (1998). Predictors, causes, and correlates of male youth violence. In M. Tonry & M. H. Moore (Eds.), *Crime and justice: A review of research* (Vol. 24, pp. 421–475). Chicago: The University of Chicago Press.

Farrington, D. P., Ohlin, L., & Wilson, J. Q. (1986). *Understanding and controlling crime: Toward a new research strategy.* New York: Springer-Verlag.

Farrington, D. P., Osborn, S. G., & West, D. J. (1978). The persistence of labeling effects. *British Journal of Criminology, 18,* 277–284.

Faust, F. L., & Brantingham, P. J. (1979). *Juvenile justice philosophy.* St. Paul, MN: West Publishing.

Federal Bureau of Investigation (1997). *Uniform crime reports for the United States.* Washington, DC: U.S. Government Printing Office.

Federal Bureau of Investigation (2002). *Uniform crime reports for the United States.* Washington, DC: U.S. Government Printing Office.

Feiler, S. M., & Sheley, J. F. (1999). Legal and racial elements of public willingness to transfer juvenile offenders to adult court. *Journal of Criminal Justice, 27*(1), 55–64.

Feld, B. C. (1987). The juvenile court meets the principle of the offense: Legislative changes in juvenile waiver statutes. *The Journal of Criminal Law and Criminology, 78*(3), 471–533.

Feld, B. C. (1988). *In re Gault* revisited: A cross-state comparison of the right to counsel in juvenile court. *Crime & Delinquency, 34,* 393–424.

Feld, B. C. (1989). Bad law makes hard cases: Reflections on teen-aged axe-murderers, judicial activism, and legislative default. *Journal of Law and Inequality*, 8(1), 1–101.

Feld, B. C. (1993). Criminalizing the American juvenile court. In M. Tonry (Ed.), *Crime and justice: A review of research* (Vol. 17, pp. 197–280). Chicago: The University of Chicago Press.

Feld, B. C. (1998a). Abolish the juvenile court: Youthfulness, criminal responsibility, and sentencing policy. *The Journal of Criminal Law and Criminology*, 88(1), 68–136.

Feld, B. C. (1998b). Juvenile and criminal justice systems' responses to youth violence. In M. Tonry & M. H. Moore (Eds.), *Crime and justice: A review of research* (Vol. 24, pp. 189–261). Chicago: The University of Chicago Press.

Feld, B. C. (2000). Legislative exclusion of offenses from juvenile court jurisdiction: A history and critique. In J. Fagan & F. E. Zimring (Eds.), *The changing borders of juvenile justice: Transfer of adolescents to the criminal court* (pp. 83–144). Chicago: The University of Chicago Press.

Flaherty, M. (1980). *An assessment of the incidence of juvenile suicide in adult jails, lock-ups, and juvenile detention centers*. Champaign, IL: Community Research Forum.

Forst, M. L., & Blomquist, M. E. (1991). Cracking down on juveniles: The changing ideology of youth corrections. *Notre Dame Journal of Law, Ethics & Public Policy*, 5, 323–375.

Forst, M., Fagan, J., & Vivona, T. S. (1989). Youths in prisons and training schools: Perceptions and consequences of the treatment-custody dichotomy. *Juvenile and Family Court Journal*, 40, 1–14.

Frazier, C. E., & Cochran, J. C. (1986). Detention of juveniles: Its effects on subsequent juvenile court processing decisions. *Youth and Society*, 17, 286–305.

Fried, C. S., & Reppucci, N. D. (2001). Criminal decision making: The development of adolescent judgment, criminal responsibility, and culpability. *Law and Human Behavior*, 25(1), 45–61.

Fritsch, E. J., Caeti, T. J., & Hemmens, C. (1996). Spare the needle but not the punishment: The incarceration of waived youth in Texas prisons. *Crime & Delinquency*, 42(4), 593–609.

Fritsch, E. J., & Hemmens, C. (1995). Juvenile waiver in the United States 1979–1995: A comparison and analysis of state waiver statutes. *Juvenile and Family Court Journal*, 46, 17–35.

Frost Clausel, L. E., & Bonnie, R. J. (2000). Juvenile justice on appeal. In J. Fagan & F. E. Zimring (Eds.), *The changing borders of juvenile justice: Transfer of adolescents to the criminal court* (pp. 181–206). Chicago: The University of Chicago Press.

Gaarder, E., & Belknap, J. (2002). Tenuous borders: Girls transferred to adult court. *Criminology*, 40(3), 481–517.

Gaes, G. G. (1998). Correctional treatment. In M. Tonry (Ed.), *The handbook of crime and punishment* (pp. 712–738). New York: Oxford University Press.

Gendreau, P., Goggin, C., & Smith, P. (1999). The forgotten issue in effective correctional treatment: Program implementation. *International Journal of Offender Therapy and Comparative Criminology*, 43(2), 180–187.

Gendreau, P., Little, T., & Goggin, C. (1996). A meta-analysis of the predictors of adult offender recidivism: What works! *Criminology*, 34(4), 575–607.

Gendreau, P., & Ross, R. R. (1987). Revivification of rehabilitation: Evidence from the 1980s. *Justice Quarterly*, 4(3), 349–407.

Geraghty, T. F. (1998). Justice for children: How do we get there? *The Journal of Criminal Law and Criminology*, 88(8), 190–241.

Gibbons, D. C. (1999). Changing lawbreakers—What have we learned since the 1950s? *Crime & Delinquency*, 45(2), 272–293.

Gibbs, J. P. (1968). Crime, punishment, and deterrence. *Southwestern Social Science Quarterly*, 48, 515–530.

Gibbs, J. P. (1975). *Crime, punishment, and deterrence*. New York: Elsevier.

Gillespie, L. K., & Norman, M. D. (1984). Does certification mean prison: Some preliminary findings from Utah. *Juvenile and Family Court Journal*, 35, 23–34.

Gold, M., & Williams, J. R. (1969). National study of the aftermath of apprehension. *Prospectus*, 3, 3–19.

Gottfredson, D. C., & Barton, W. H. (1993). Deinstitutionalization of juvenile offenders. *Criminology*, 31(4), 591–607.

Grasmick, H. G., & Bursik, R. J. (1990). Conscience, significant others, and rational choice: Extending the deterrence model. *Law & Society Review*, 24(3), 837–861.

Greenbaum, S. (1997). Kids and guns: From playgrounds to battlegrounds. *Juvenile Justice*, III(2), 3–10.

Greenberg, M., & Feinberg, M. (2002, January 29). *An evaluation of PCCD's Communities That Care Delinquency Prevention Initiative*. Retrieved October 6, 2002, from http://www.pccd.state.pa.us.

Greenwood, P. W. (1995). Juvenile crime and juvenile justice. In J. Q. Wilson & J. Petersilia (Eds.), *Crime* (pp. 91–117). San Francisco: Institute for Contemporary Studies.

Griffin, P. (2003). *Trying and sentencing juveniles as adults: An analysis of state transfer and blended sentencing laws.* Pittsburgh, PA: National Center for Juvenile Justice.

Griffin, P., Torbet, P., & Szymanski, L. (1998). *Trying juveniles as adults in criminal court: An analysis of state transfer provisions.* Washington, DC: Office of Juvenile Justice and Delinquency Prevention.

Hagan, J., & Bumiller, K. (1983). Making sense of sentencing: A review and critique of sentencing research. In A. Blumstein, J. Cohen, S. E. Martin, & M. Tonry (Eds.), *Research on sentencing: The search for reform* (pp. 1–54). Washington, DC: National Academy Press.

Hagedorn, J. M. (1998). Gang violence in the postindustrial era. In M. Tonry & M. H. Moore (Eds.), *Crime and justice: A review of research* (Vol. 24, pp. 365–419). Chicago: The University of Chicago Press.

Hamparian, D., Estep, L. K., Muntean, S. M., Prestino, R., Swisher, R. G., Wallace, P. L., et al. (1982). *Youth in adult court: Between two worlds.* Columbus, OH: Academy for Contemporary Problems.

Harrison, P. M., & Karberg, J. (2004). *Prison and jail inmates at midyear 2003* (Report No. NCJ 203947). Washington, DC: U.S. Department of Justice.

Hartman, M. (2003). *Annual statistical report 2002.* Camp Hill, PA: Pennsylvania Department of Corrections.

Hawkins, D., Arthur, M. W., & Catalano, R. F. (1995). Preventing substance abuse. In M. Tonry & D. P. Farrington (Eds.), *Building a safer society: Strategic approaches to crime prevention* (pp. 343–427). Chicago: The University of Chicago Press.

Hawkins, D., Herrenkohl, T., Farrington, D. P., Brewer, D., Catalano, R. F., & Harachi, T. W. (1999). A review of predictors of youth violence. In R. Loeber & D. P. Farrington (Eds.), *Serious and violent juvenile offenders: Risk factors and successful interventions* (pp. 106–146). Thousand Oaks, CA: Sage Publications.

Houghtalin, M., & Mays, G. L. (1991). Criminal dispositions of New Mexico juveniles transferred to adult court. *Crime & Delinquency, 37*(3), 393–407.

Howell, J. C. (1996). Juvenile transfers to the criminal justice system: State of the art. *Law & Policy, 18*(1 & 2), 17–60.

Howell, J. C. (1997). *Juvenile justice and youth violence.* Thousand Oaks, CA: Sage Publications.

Howell, J. C. (2003). *Preventing & reducing juvenile delinquency: A comprehensive framework*. Thousand Oaks, CA: Sage Publications.

Howell, J. C., & Hawkins, J. D. (1998). Prevention of youth violence. In M. Tonry & M. H. Moore (Eds.), *Crime and justice: A review of research* (Vol. 24, pp. 263–313). Chicago: The University of Chicago Press.

Howell, J. C., Krisberg, B., Hawkins, J. D., & Wilson, J. J. (1995). *A sourcebook: Serious, violent, and chronic juvenile offenders*. Thousand Oaks, CA: Sage Publications.

In re Gault, 387 U.S. 1 (1967).

In re Winship, 397 U.S. 358 (1970).

Jacobs, M. D. (1990). *Screwing the system and making it work*. Chicago: The University of Chicago Press.

Jensen, E. J., & Metsger, L. K. (1994). A test of the deterrent effect of legislative waiver on violent juvenile crime. *Crime & Delinquency, 40*(1), 96–104.

Johnson, K. (2004, July 21). Mean streets once again: Gang activity surging. *USA Today*, pp. 1A, 2A.

Jonas, M. (2004, August 15). *As violence flares, a call for hard cash*. Retrieved September 3, 2004, from http://www.boston.com.news/local/massachusetts/articles.

Jones, S., & Roberts, L. (1998, July 2). *The case of Nathaniel Abraham: Background to the prosecution of a child for murder*. Retrieved July 23, 2003, from http://www.wsws.org.

Keiter, R. B. (1973). Criminal or delinquent? A study of juvenile cases transferred to the criminal court. *Crime & Delinquency, 19*, 528–538.

Kent v. United States, 383 U.S. 541 (1966).

Kinder, K., Veneziano, C., Fichter, M., & Azuma, H. (1995). A comparison of the dispositions of juvenile offenders certified as adults with juvenile offenders not certified. *Juvenile and Family Court Journal, 46*, 37–42.

Klein, M. W. (1986). Labeling theory and delinquency policy: An experimental test. *Criminal Justice and Behavior, 13*(1), 47–79.

Klemke, L. W. (1978). Does apprehension for shoplifting amplify or terminate shoplifting activity? *Law & Society Review, 12*, 391–403.

Klepper, S., & Nagin, D. (1989). The deterrent effect of perceived certainty and severity of punishment revisited. *Criminology, 27*(4), 721–746.

Krebs, J. (1995, November 1). Ridge hails anti-crime arsenal: Democrats feel politics buried in their proposals. *The Patriot-News*, p. A1.

Krisberg, B., & Austin, J. F. (1993). *Reinventing juvenile justice*. Newbury Park, CA: Sage Publications.

Krisberg, B., Austin, J. F., & Steele, P. A. (1989). *Unlocking juvenile corrections*. San Francisco: National Council on Crime and Delinquency.

Krisberg, B., Currie, E., Onek, D., & Wiebush, R. G. (1995). Graduated sanctions for serious, violent, and chronic juvenile offenders. In J. C. Howell, B. Krisberg, J. D. Hawkins, & J. J. Wilson (Eds.), *A sourcebook: Serious, violent, & chronic juvenile offenders* (pp. 142–170). Thousand Oaks, CA: Sage Publications.

Lab, S. P., & Whitehead, J. T. (1988). An analysis of juvenile correctional treatment. *Crime & Delinquency, 34*(1), 60–83.

Lanza-Kaduce, L., & Radosevich, M. J. (1987). Negative reactions to processing and substance use among young incarcerated males. *Deviant Behavior, 8*, 137–148.

Lee, L. (1994). Factors determining waiver in a juvenile court. *Journal of Criminal Justice, 22*(4), 329–339.

Lemert, E. M. (1951). *Social pathology: A systematic approach to the theory of sociopathic behavior*. New York: McGraw-Hill.

Lemert, E. M. (1972). *Human deviance, social problems, and social control* (2nd ed.). Englewood Cliffs, NJ: Prentice-Hall.

Lemmon, J. H., Sontheimer, H., & Saylor, K. A. (1991). *A study of Pennsylvania juveniles transferred to criminal court in 1986*. Harrisburg, PA: The Pennsylvania Juvenile Court Judges' Commission.

Leonard, K. K., Pope, C. E., & Feyerherm, W. H. (1995). *Minorities in juvenile justice*. Thousand Oaks, CA: Sage Publications.

Levitt, S. D. (1998). Juvenile crime and punishment. *Journal of Political Economy, 106*(6), 1156–1185.

Lipsey, M. W. (1992). Juvenile delinquency treatment: A meta-analytic inquiry into the variability of effects. In D. T. Cook, H. Cooper, D. S. Cordray, H. Hartman, L. V. Hedges, R. J. Knight, et al. (Eds.), *Meta-analysis for explanation* (pp. 83–127). New York: Russell Sage Foundation.

Lipsey, M. W. (1995). What do we learn from 400 research studies on the effectiveness of treatment with juvenile delinquents? In J. McGuire (Ed.), *What works? Reducing offending* (pp. 63–78). New York: John Wiley.

Lipsey, M. W. (1999). Can intervention rehabilitate serious delinquents? *Annals of the American Academy of Political and Social Science, 564*, 142–156.

Lipsey, M. W., & Derzon, J. H. (1999). Predictors of violent or serious delinquency in adolescence and early adulthood: A synthesis of longitudinal research. In R. Loeber & D. P. Farrington (Eds.), *Serious and violent juvenile offenders: Risk factors and successful interventions* (pp. 86–105). Thousand Oaks, CA: Sage Publications.

Lipsey, M. W., & Wilson, D. B. (1999). Effective intervention for serious juvenile offenders: A synthesis of research. In R. Loeber & D. P. Farrington (Eds.), *Serious and violent juvenile offenders: Risk factors and successful interventions* (pp. 313–345). Thousand Oaks, CA: Sage Publications.

Lipton, D., Martinson, R., & Wilks, J. (1975). *The effectiveness of correctional treatment: A survey of treatment evaluation studies.* New York: Praeger Publishers.

Loeber, R., & Farrington, D. P. (1999). *Serious & violent juvenile offenders: Risk factors and successful interventions.* Thousand Oaks, CA: Sage Publications.

Loeber, R., & LeBlanc, M. (1990). Toward a developmental criminology. In M. Tonry & N. Morris (Eds.), *Crime and justice: An annual review of research* (Vol. 12, pp. 375–473). Chicago: The University of Chicago Press.

Logan, C. H. (1975). Arrest rates and deterrence. *Social Science Quarterly, 56,* 376–389.

MacKenzie, D. L. (2002). Reducing the criminal activities of known offenders and delinquents: Crime prevention in the courts and corrections. In L. W. Sherman, D. P. Farrington, B. E. Welsh, & D. L. MacKenzie (Eds.), *Evidence-based crime prevention* (pp. 330–404). New York: Routledge.

Mahoney, A. R. (1974). The effect of labeling upon youths in the juvenile justice system: A review of the evidence. *Law & Society Review, 8,* 583–614.

Makkai, T., & Braithwaite, J. (1994). The dialectics of corporate deterrence. *Journal of Research in Crime & Delinquency, 31,* 347–373.

Maltz, M. D. (1984). *Recidivism.* Orlando, FL: Academic Press.

Martinson, R. (1974). What works? Questions and answers about prison reform. *The Public Interest, 35,* 22–54.

McKeiver v. Pennsylvania, 403 U.S. 528 (1971).

Meddis, S. V. (1993, October 29). Poll: Treat juveniles the same as adult offenders. *USA Today,* pp. A1, A11.

Merlo, A. V., & Benekos, P. J. (2000). *What's wrong with the criminal justice system? Ideology, politics, and the media.* Cincinnati, OH: Anderson Publishing Co.

Minor, K. I., Hartmann, D. J., & Terry, S. (1997). Predictors of juvenile court actions and recidivism. *Crime & Delinquency, 43*(3), 328–344.

Minor, W. W., & Harry, J. P. (1982). Deterrent and experiential effects in perceptual research: A replication and extension. *Journal of Research in Crime and Delinquency, 19,* 190–203.

Missouri court declares execution of minors unconstitutional. (2003). *Juvenile Justice Update, 9*(5), 1, 12–13.

Moore, E. A. (2000). Sentencing opinion: *People of the State of Michigan v. Nathaniel Abraham. Juvenile and Family Court Journal, 51*(2), 1–11.

Moore, M. H., & Tonry, M. (1998). Youth violence in America. In M. Tonry & M. H. Moore (Eds.), *Crime and justice: A review of research* (Vol. 24, pp. 1–26). Chicago: The University of Chicago Press.

Moore, M. H., & Wakeling, S. (1997). Juvenile justice: Shoring up the foundations. In M. Tonry (Ed.), *Crime and justice: A review of research* (Vol. 22, pp. 253–301). Chicago: The University of Chicago Press.

Morse, S. J. (1998). Immaturity and irresponsibility. *The Journal of Criminal Law and Criminology, 88*(1), 15–67.

Murray, C. A., & Cox, L. A. (1979). *Beyond probation: Juvenile corrections and the chronic delinquent.* Beverly Hills, CA: Sage Publications.

Myers, D. (1997, March). *Excluding juvenile offenders from juvenile court: The effects of Pennsylvania's recent legislation.* Paper presented at the annual meeting of the Academy of Criminal Justice Sciences, Louisville, KY.

Myers, D. L. (2001). *Excluding violent youths from juvenile court: The effectiveness of legislative waiver.* New York: LFB Scholarly Publishing.

Myers, D. L. (2003a). Adult crime, adult time: Punishing violent youth in the adult criminal justice system. *Youth Violence and Juvenile Justice: An Interdisciplinary Journal, 1*(2), 173–197.

Myers, D. L. (2003b). The house of last resort: Incarcerating juveniles in adult prisons. In S. H. Decker, L. F. Alarid, & C. M. Katz (Eds.), *Controversies in Criminal Justice* (pp. 321–329). Los Angeles: Roxbury Publishing.

Myers, D. L. (2003c). The recidivism of violent youths in juvenile and adult court: A consideration of selection bias. *Youth Violence and Juvenile Justice: An Interdisciplinary Journal, 1*(1), 79–101.

Myers, D. L., & Kiehl, K. (2001). The predispositional status of violent youthful offenders: Is there a "custody gap" in adult criminal court? *Justice Research and Policy, 3*(1), 115–143.

Nagin, D. S. (1978). General deterrence: A review of the empirical evidence. In A. Blumstein, J. Cohen, & D. Nagin (Eds.), *Deterrence and incapacitation: Estimating the effects of criminal sanctions on crime rates* (pp. 95–139). Washington, DC: National Academy of Sciences.

Nagin, D. S. (1998). Criminal deterrence research at the outset of the twenty-first century. In M. Tonry (Ed.), *Crime and justice: A review of research* (pp. 1–42). Chicago, IL: The University of Chicago Press.

Nagin, D. S., & Paternoster, R. (1993). Enduring individual differences and rational choice theories of crime. *Law & Society Review, 27*(3), 467–496.

National Council of Juvenile and Family Court Judges. (1998). *The Janiculum Project: Structural, procedural, and programmatic recommendations for the future juvenile court.* Reno, NV: National Council of Juvenile and Family Court Judges.

Office of Juvenile Justice and Delinquency Prevention. (2002). *2001 Report to Congress: Title V community prevention grants program.* Fairfax, VA: Caliber Associates.

Parent, D., Leiter, V., Livens, L., Wentworth, D., & Stephen, K. (1994). *Criminal victimization in the United States, 2002: A national crime victimization survey report.* Washington, DC: U.S. Department of Justice.

Paternoster, R. (1987). The deterrent effect of the perceived certainty and severity of punishment: A review of the evidence and issues. *Justice Quarterly, 4*(2), 173–217.

Paternoster, R. (1989a). Absolute and restrictive deterrence in a panel of youth: Explaining the onset, persistence/desistence, and frequency of delinquent offending. *Social Problems, 36*(3), 289–309.

Paternoster, R. (1989b). Decisions to participate in and desist from four types of common delinquency: Deterrence and the rational choice perspective. *Law & Society Review, 23*(1), 7–40.

Paternoster, R. (1991). *Capital Punishment in America.* New York: Lexington Books.

Paternoster, R., Brame, R., Bachman, R., & Sherman, L. W. (1997). Do fair procedures matter? The effect of procedural justice on spouse assault. *Law & Society Review, 31*, 163–204.

Paternoster, R., & Iovanni, L. (1986). The deterrent effect of perceived severity: A reexamination. *Social Forces, 64*, 751–777.

Paternoster, R., & Iovanni, L. (1989). The labeling perspective and delinquency: An elaboration of the theory and an assessment of the evidence. *Justice Quarterly, 6*(3), 359–394.

Paternoster, R., & Piquero, A. (1995). Reconceptualizing deterrence: An empirical test of personal and vicarious experiences. *Journal of Research in Crime and Delinquency, 32*(3), 251286.

Paternoster, R., Saltzman, L. E., Chiricos, T. G., & Waldo, G. P. (1982). Perceived risk and deterrence: Methodological artifacts in perceptual deterrence research. *The Journal of Criminal Law and Criminology, 73*, 1238–1258.

Paternoster, R., Saltzman, L. E., Waldo, G. P., & Chiricos, T. G. (1983). Estimating perceptual stability and deterrent effects: The role of perceived legal punishment in the inhibition of criminal involvement. *The Journal of Criminal Law and Criminology, 74*, 270–297.

Pennsylvania Juvenile Court Judges' Commission. (1992/1996). *The Juvenile Act.* (Rev.) 42 PA C.S. Sec. 6301 et seq. Harrisburg, PA: Juvenile Court Judges' Commission.

Piliavin, I., Gartner, R., Thorton, C., & Matsueda, R. (1986). Crime, deterrence, and rational choice. *American Sociological Review, 51*, 101–119.

Piquero, A., & Tibbetts, S. (1996). Specifying the direct and indirect effects of low self-control and situational factors in offenders' decision making: Toward a more complete model of rational offending. *Justice Quarterly, 13*(3), 481–510.

Pisciotta, A. W. (1994). A retrospective look at the task force report on juvenile delinquency and youth crime. In J. A. Conley (Ed.), *The 1967 President's Crime Commission Report: Its impact 25 years later* (pp. 81–99). Cincinnati, OH: Anderson Publishing.

Platt, A. (1969). *The child savers.* Chicago: The University of Chicago Press.

Podkopacz, M. R., & Feld, B. C. (1996). The end of the line: An empirical study of judicial waiver. *The Journal of Criminal Law and Criminology, 86*(2), 449–492.

Pope, C. E., & Feyerherm, W. H. (1990). Minority status and juvenile justice processing: An assessment of the research literature. *Criminal Justice Abstracts, 22*, 327–336, 527–542.

Poulos, T. M., & Orchowsky, S. (1994). Serious juvenile offenders: Predicting the probability of transfer to criminal court. *Crime & Delinquency, 40*(1), 3–17.

President's Commission on Law Enforcement and Administration of Justice. (1967). *The challenge of crime in a free society.* Washington, DC: U.S. Government Printing Office.

Puzzanchera, C. M. (2003). *Delinquency cases waived to criminal court, 1990–1999* (Report No. FS-200304). Washington, DC: Office of Juvenile Justice and Delinquency Prevention.

Rainville, G. A., & Smith, S. K. (2003). *Juvenile felony defendants in criminal courts* (Report No. NCJ 197961). Washington, DC: Bureau of Justice Statistics.

Redding, R. E. (2003). The effects of adjudicating and sentencing juveniles as adults. *Youth Violence and Juvenile Justice: An Interdisciplinary Journal, 1*(2), 128–155.

Redding, R. E., & Howell, J. C. (2000). Blended sentencing in American juvenile courts. In J. Fagan & F. E. Zimring (Eds.), *The changing borders of juvenile justice: Transfer of adolescents to the criminal court* (pp. 145–180). Chicago: The University of Chicago Press.

Reddington, F. P., & Sapp, A. D. (1997). Juveniles in adult prisons: Problems and prospects. *Journal of Crime and Justice, 20*(2), 139–152.

Regnery, A. S. (1985). Getting away with murder: Why the juvenile system needs an overhaul. *Policy Review, 34*, 65–68.

Regnery, A. S. (1986). A federal perspective on juvenile justice reform. *Crime & Delinquency, 32*(1), 39–51.

Reiss, A. J., Jr. (1994). An evaluation and assessment of the impact of the Task Force Report: Crime and Its Impact—An Assessment. In J. A. Conley (Ed.), *The 1967 President's Crime Commission Report: Its impact 25 years later* (pp. 1–20). Cincinnati, OH: Anderson Publishing.

Rendleman, D. R. (1979). *Parens patriae*: From chancery to the juvenile court. In F. L. Faust & P. J. Brantingham (Eds.), *Juvenile justice philosophy* (pp. 58–96). St. Paul, MN: West Publishing.

Risler, E. A., Sweatman, T., & Nackerud, L. (1998). Evaluating the Georgia legislative waiver's effectiveness in deterring juvenile crime. *Research on Social Work Practice, 8*, 657–667.

Roper v. Simmons, 124 S. Ct. 1171 (2004).

Rothman, D. J. (1980). *Conscience and convenience: The asylum and its alternatives in progressive America*. Boston: Little, Brown.

Royscher, M., & Edelman, P. (1981). Treating juveniles as adults in New York: What does it mean and how is it working? In J. C. Hall, D. M. Hamparian, J. M. Pettibone, & J. L. White (Eds.), *Major issues in juvenile justice information and training: Readings in public policy* (pp. 265–293). Columbus, OH: Academy for Contemporary Problems.

Rudman, C., Hartstone, E., Fagan, J., & Moore, M. (1986). Violent youth in adult court: Process and punishment. *Crime & Delinquency, 32*(1), 75–96.

Sagatun, I., McCollum, L. L., & Edwards, L. (1985). The effect of transfers from juvenile to criminal court: A loglinear analysis. *Journal of Crime and Justice, 8,* 65–92.

Saltzman, L. E., Paternoster, R., Waldo, G. P., & Chiricos, T. G. (1982). Deterrent and experiential effects: The problem of causal order in perceptual deterrence research. *Journal of Research in Crime and Delinquency, 19,* 172–189.

Sampson, P. (1995a, April 2). Bill would expose crimes to media, public. *Sunday Patriot-News,* p. A6.

Sampson, P. (1995b, October 26). Senate addresses youth crimes: Serious offenses could bring automatic transfer to adult court. *The Patriot-News,* p. B5.

Sanborn, J. B. (1994). Certification to criminal court: The important policy questions of how, when, and why. *Crime & Delinquency, 40*(2), 262–281.

Sanborn, J. B. (2003). Hard choices or obvious ones? Developing policy for excluding youth from juvenile court. *Youth Violence and Juvenile Justice: An Interdisciplinary Journal, 1*(2), 198–214.

Schall v. Martin, 467 U.S. 253 (1984).

Schneider, A. L., & Ervin, L. (1990). Specific deterrence, rational choice, and decision heuristics: Applications in juvenile justice. *Social Science Quarterly, 71*(3), 585–601.

Schwartz, I. M. (1989). *(In)justice for juveniles.* Lexington, MA: Lexington Books.

Schwartz, I. M., Guo, S., & Kerbs, J. J. (1993). The impact of demographic variables on public opinion regarding juvenile justice: Implications for public policy. *Crime & Delinquency, 39*(1), 5–28.

Scott, E. S., & Grisso, T. (1998). The evolution of adolescence: A developmental perspective on juvenile justice reform. *The Journal of Criminal Law and Criminology, 88*(1), 137–189.

Sechrest, L., White, S. O., & Brown, E. D. (1979). *The rehabilitation of criminal offenders: Problems and prospects.* Washington, DC: National Academy of Sciences.

Shannon, L. W. (1980). Assessing the relationship of adult criminal careers to juvenile careers. In C. Abt (Ed.), *Problems in American social policy* (pp. 232–246). Cambridge, MA: Abt Books.

Sherman, L. W. (1992). *Policing domestic violence: Experiments and dilemmas.* New York: Free Press.

Sherman, L. W. (1993). Defiance, deterrence, and irrelevance: A theory of the criminal sanction. *Journal of Research in Crime and Delinquency, 30*(4), 445–473.

Sherman, L. W., Farrington, D. P., Welsh, B. C., & MacKenzie, D. L. (2002). *Evidence-based crime prevention.* New York: Routledge.

Sherman, L. W., Gottfredson, D., MacKenzie, D., Eck, J., Reuter, P., & Bushway, S. (1997). *Preventing crime: What works, what doesn't, what's promising.* Washington, DC: US Department of Justice.

Sherman, L. W., & Smith, D. A. (1992). Crime, punishment, and stake in conformity: Legal and informal control of domestic violence. *American Sociological Review, 57,* 680–690.

Sickmund, M. (2003). *Juveniles in court* (Report No. NCJ 195420). Washington, DC: Office of Juvenile Justice and Delinquency Prevention.

Sickmund, M., Snyder, H. N., & Poe-Yamagata, E. (1997). *Juvenile offenders and victims: 1997 update on violence* (Report No. NCJ 165703). Washington, DC: Office of Juvenile Justice and Delinquency Prevention.

Silverman, I. J. (2001). *Corrections: A comprehensive view* (2nd ed.). Belmont, CA: Wadsworth.

Singer, S. I. (1993). The automatic waiver of juveniles and substantive justice. *Crime & Delinquency, 39*(2), 253–261.

Singer, S. I. (1996). *Recriminalizing delinquency: Violent juvenile crime and juvenile justice reform.* New York: Cambridge University Press.

Singer, S. I. (2003). Incarcerating juveniles into adulthood: Organizational fields of knowledge and the back end of waiver. *Youth Violence and Juvenile Justice: An Interdisciplinary Journal, 1*(2), 115–127.

Singer, S. I., & McDowall, D. (1988). Criminalizing delinquency: The deterrent effects of the New York juvenile offender law. *Law & Society Review, 22*(3), 521–535.

Smalley, S. (2004, August 6). *Youth violence is sharply on rise (Boston Globe).* Retrieved September 3, 2004, from http://www.boston.com.news/local/massachusetts/articles.

Smith, B. (1998). Children in custody: 20-year trends in juvenile detention, correctional, and shelter facilities. *Crime & Delinquency, 44*(4), 526–543.

Smith, D. A. (1986). The neighborhood context of police behavior. In A. Reiss & M. Tonry (Eds.), *Crime and justice: An annual review of research* (Vol. 8, pp. 313–341). Chicago: The University of Chicago Press.

Smith, D. A., & Gartin, P. R. (1989). Specifying specific deterrence: The influence of arrest on future criminal activity. *American Sociological Review, 54*, 94–105.

Smith, D. A., & Paternoster, R. (1990). Formal processing and future delinquency: Deviance amplification as a selection artifact. *Law & Society Review, 24*(5), 1109–1131.

Snyder, H. N. (2002). *Juvenile arrests 2000* (Report No. NCJ 191729). Washington, DC: Office of Juvenile Justice and Delinquency Prevention.

Snyder, H. N., & Sickmund, M. (1995). *Juvenile offenders and victims: A national report* (Report No. NCJ 153569). Washington, DC: Office of Juvenile Justice and Delinquency Prevention.

Snyder, H. N., & Sickmund, M. (1999). *Juvenile offenders and victims: 1999 national report* (Report No. NCJ 178257). Washington, DC: Office of Juvenile Justice and Delinquency Prevention.

Snyder, H. N., Sickmund, M., & Poe-Yamagata, E. (2000). *Juvenile transfers to criminal court in the 1990s: Lessons learned from four studies* (Report No. NCJ 181301). Washington, DC: Office of Juvenile Justice and Delinquency Prevention.

Sprott, J. B. (1998). Understanding public opposition to a separate youth justice system. *Crime & Delinquency, 44*(3), 399–411.

Stafford, M. C., & Warr, M. (1993). A reconceptualization of general and specific deterrence. *Journal of Research in Crime and Delinquency, 30*(2), 123–135.

Stanford v. Kentucky, 492 U.S. 361 (1989).

Stanley, B. (1996, November 17). States strengthen laws to crack down on juvenile crime: Now it's easier to try youths as adults across nation; impact unclear. *Sunday Patriot-News*, p. A4.

State ex rel. Christopher Simmons v. Roper, SC84454 (2003).

Steinberg, L., & Cauffman, E. (1996). Maturity of judgment in adolescence: Psychosocial factors in adolescent decision-making. *Law and Human Behavior, 20*(3), 249–272.

Stojkovic, S. (1994). The President's Crime Commission recommendations for corrections: The twilight of the idols. In J. A. Conley (Ed.), *The 1967 President's Crime Commission Report: Its impact 25 years later* (pp. 37–55). Cincinnati, OH: Anderson Publishing.

Strom, K. J., Smith, S. K., & Snyder, H. N. (1998). *Juvenile felony defendants in criminal courts* (NCJ 165815). Washington, DC: Bureau of Justice Statistics and the Office of Juvenile Justice and Delinquency Prevention.

Sutton, J. (1988). *Stubborn children: Controlling delinquency in the United States.* Berkeley, CA: University of California Press.

Tanenhaus, D. S. (2000). The evolution of transfer out of the juvenile court. In J. Fagan & F. E. Zimring (Eds.), *The changing borders of juvenile justice: Transfer of adolescents to the criminal court* (pp. 13–43). Chicago: The University of Chicago Press.

Tannenbaum, F. (1938). *Crime and the community.* New York: Columbia University Press.

Thomas, C. W., & Bilchik, S. (1985). Prosecuting juveniles in criminal courts: A legal and empirical analysis. *The Journal of Criminal Law and Criminology, 76*(2), 439–479.

Thomas, C. W., & Bishop, D. (1984). The effect of formal and informal sanctions on delinquency: A longitudinal comparison of labeling and deterrence theories. *The Journal of Criminal Law and Criminology, 75*(4), 1222–1245.

Thompson v. Oklahoma, 487 U.S. 815 (1988).

Thornberry, T. P., Huizinga, D., & Loeber, R. (1995). The prevention of serious delinquency and violence: Implications from the program of research on the causes and correlates of delinquency. In J. C. Howell, B. Krisberg, J. D. Hawkins, & J. J. Wilson (Eds.), *A sourcebook: Serious, violent, and chronic juvenile offenders* (pp. 213–237). Thousand Oaks, CA: Sage Publications.

Tittle, C. R. (1969). Crime rates and legal sanctions. *Social Problems, 16,* 408–423.

Tittle, C. R., & Rowe, A. R. (1974). Certainty of arrest and crime rates: A further test of the deterrence hypothesis. *Social Forces, 52,* 455–462.

Tonry, M. (1996). *Sentencing matters.* New York: Oxford University Press.

Tonry, M. (1998). Crime and punishment in America. In M. Tonry (Ed.), *The handbook of crime and punishment* (pp. 3–27). New York: Oxford University Press.

Torbet, P., Gable, R., Hurst, H. I., Montgomery, I., Szymanski, L., & Thomas, D. (1996). *State responses to serious and violent juvenile crime* (Report No. NCJ 161565). Washington, DC: Office of Juvenile Justice and Delinquency Prevention.

Torbet, P., Griffin, P., Hurst, H., & MacKenzie, L. R. (2000). *Juveniles facing criminal sanctions: Three states that changed the rules.* Washington, DC: Office of Juvenile Justice and Delinquency Prevention.

Torbet, P., & Szymanski, L. (1998). *State legislative responses to violent juvenile crime: 1996–1997 update.* Washington, DC: Office of Juvenile Justice and Delinquency Prevention.

Triplett, R. (1996). The growing threat: Gangs and juvenile offenders. In T. J. Flanagan & D. R. Longmire (Eds.), *Americans view crime and justice: A national public opinion survey.* Thousand Oaks, CA: Sage Publications.

Tyler, T. R. (1990). *Why people obey the law.* New Haven, CT: Yale University Press.

Vogel, B. L., & Vogel, R. E. (2003). The age of death: Appraising public opinion of juvenile capital punishment. *Journal of Criminal Justice, 31,* 169–183.

Wells, R. (2002, January 9). Graduation caps SCI Pine Grove's first year. *Indiana Gazette,* pp. 1, 12.

Whitehead, J. T., & Lab, S. P. (1989). A meta-analysis of juvenile correctional treatment. *Journal of Research in Crime and Delinquency, 26*(3), 276–295.

White Stack, B. (2001, November 23). Adult time prison too big: Indiana County teen lockup has hundreds of vacant beds. *Pittsburgh Post-Gazette,* pp. B1, B5.

Wilkins v. Missouri, 492 U.S. 361 (1989).

Wilson, J. J. (2000). *Juveniles and the death penalty* (Report No. NCJ 184748). Washington, DC: Office of Juvenile Justice and Delinquency Prevention.

Wilson, J. Q. (1975/1983). *Thinking about crime.* (Rev. ed.). New York: Basic Books.

Wilson, J. Q. (1995). Crime and public policy. In J. Q. Wilson & J. Petersilia (Eds.), *Crime* (pp. 489–507). San Francisco: Institute for Contemporary Studies.

Winner, L., Lanza-Kaduce, L., Bishop, D. M., & Frazier, C. E. (1997). The transfer of juveniles to criminal court: Reexamining recidivism over the long term. *Crime & Delinquency, 43*(4), 548–563.

Wolfgang, M. (1982). Abolish the juvenile court system. *California Lawyer, 2,* 12–13.

Wolfgang, M., Figlio, R., & Sellin, T. (1972). *Delinquency in a birth cohort.* Chicago: The University of Chicago Press.

Wong, S. C., Catalano, R. F., Hawkins, J. D., & Chappell, P. J. (1996). *Communities That Care: A comprehensive prevention program.* Seattle, WA: Developmental Research and Programs, Inc.

Wooldredge, J. D. (1988). Differentiating the effects of juvenile court sentences on eliminating recidivism. *Journal of Research in Crime and Delinquency, 25*(3), 264–300.

Young, M. (2000). *Providing effective representation for youth prosecuted as adults* (Report No. NCJ 182502). Washington, DC: Bureau of Justice Assistance.

Zimmerman, S., Myers, D., Giever, D., Dandeneau, C., Gido, R., Kiehl, K., et al. (2000). Establishing a research institution: The partnership between IUP and the Pine Grove Prison for violent youthful offenders. *Journal for Juvenile Justice and Detention Services, 15*(2), 67–82.

Zimring, F. E. (1991). The treatment of hard cases in American juvenile justice: In defense of discretionary waiver. *Notre Dame Journal of Law, Ethics & Public Policy, 5,* 267–280.

Zimring, F. E. (1998). *American youth violence.* New York: Oxford University Press.

Zimring, F. E. (2000). The punitive necessity of waiver. In J. Fagan & F. E. Zimring (Eds.), *The changing borders of juvenile justice: Transfer of adolescents to the criminal court* (pp. 207–224). Chicago: The University of Chicago Press.

Zimring, F. E., & Hawkins, G. J. (1973). *Deterrence: The legal threat in crime control.* Chicago: The University of Chicago Press.

Index

About the Author

DAVID L. MYERS is Associate Professor of Criminology and a Dean's Associate in the School of Graduate Studies and Research at Indiana University of Pennsylvania, where he also directs the Doctoral Program in Criminology and the Center for Research in Criminology. He is a member of the IUP Research Institute Advisory Board and the Institutional Review Board of the National Center for Juvenile Justice, as well as an Associate Editor and Columnist for Criminal Justice Research Reports. He is the author of *Excluding Violent Youths from Juvenile Court: The Effectiveness of Legislative Waiver* (2001), and his articles have appeared in such journals as *Youth Violence and Juvenile Justice, Journal of Juvenile Justice and Detention Services, Criminal Justice Review, Justice Research and Policy,* and *Criminal Justice Studies.*